UNTITLED PASSAGES
BY HENRI MICHAUX

UNTITLED PASSAGES
BY HENRI MICHAUX

Edited by

Catherine de Zegher

Interview by

John Ashbery

Essays by

Raymond Bellour

Laurent Jenny

Florian Rodari

Richard Sieburth

The Drawing Center, New York

MERRELL

Published on the occasion of the exhibition
Untitled Passages by Henri Michaux
curated by Catherine de Zegher and Florian Rodari
at The Drawing Center, New York,
October 28 – December 20, 2000

This publication has been made possible with the assistance of the Getty Grant Program.

Support for the exhibition and publication has also been received from
The Eugene V. and Claire Thaw Charitable Trust,
The Michel David-Weill Foundation,
The Cultural Services of the French Embassy, New York,
and agnès b.

CONTENTS

TO DRAW THE FLOW OF TIME

Henri Michaux

Before taking up drawing I had a desire that no doubt stood in the way and that absolutely had to be realized beforehand. It seemed to correspond to my true needs and even to a general need.

Instead of one vision to the exclusion of others, I wanted to draw the moments that end to end make life, to show the inner phrase, the wordless phrase, the sinuous strand that unwinds indefinitely and is intimately present in each inner and outer event.

I wanted to draw the consciousness of existing and the flow of time. As one takes one's pulse. Or again, more modestly, that which appears when, in the evening, the film that has been exposed to the day's images, but shorter and muted, is rerun.

Cinematic drawing.

True, I was attached to my own. But how happy I would have been to see a line plotted by someone else and to be able to read in it the ins and outs of another's life, just like running my hands along a marvelous string, discovering its knots and secrets.

My own particular film was scarcely more than one or two or three lines meeting up here and there with a few others, now forming a thicket, now a plait, further on joining battle, rolling into a ball or—feelings and monuments naturally intermingled—rising up, arrogance, pride, or castle or tower ... that could be seen, that I thought should have been seen but that, to tell the truth, almost no one saw.

Intrigued, people looked at my pages and asked me what kind of 'art' was that. I tore them up. I had been made to doubt too much of their communicability. A few individuals had in that writing become interested in groups of lines here and there, tiny crossroads of impressionability and event, which they called signs, urging me even to make a dictionary of them. They were still not interested in them as a sequential development. The cinema had not yet been in existence for long.

One day a publisher, who wished to reproduce some of them on account of a certain charm he found in them, said to me: "All you have to do is make them bigger."

Annoyed—for can writing be enlarged?—I seized hold of a brush (which was destined to replace the fine-nibbed pen) so as straightaway to demonstrate that the scandalous operation was impossible.

As I drew the first lines I felt, to my extreme surprise, that something that had always been closed had opened up in me, and that this breach was to afford an outlet for a mass of movements.

The fullness of the gesture necessitated by the characters that were supposed to come out bigger had changed the spirit of the drawing. Instead of characters, instead of notations of an undefinable 'something,' they became propulsion, participation, released torrent.

Through amplitude I was able to communicate with my own speed, and in so doing I forgot what I was supposed to be about and changed my original focus.

There thus thronged into view a mass of movements of which I was full, overflowing, and had been for years. When, as a child, I engaged in daydreaming, never, so far as I remember, was I a prince and not very often a conqueror, but I was extraordinary in movements. A veritable prodigy in movements. Proteus through movements. Movements of which, in fact, no trace was visible in my attitude and which could not have been suspected, except on account of a certain air of absence and my ability to cut myself off.

Animals and I, we had dealings together. My movements, I mentally changed for theirs and, by that means, released from the limitation of being two-footed, I expanded beyond myself ... I became inebriated with them, especially with those that were outstandingly wild, sudden, and jerky. I invented impossible ones and I brought in man, not with his four limbs just about good enough for sport, but supplied with extraordinary prolongations, spontaneously prompted by his moods, his desires, in an incessant morpho-creation.

This, still alive, asked but to come into my drawings and rushed in at once. I filled hundreds of pages with the sudden release of supernumerary arms and legs and dancing movements without however managing those that in my imagination I had so easily practiced and achieved for years. Drawing was less familiar to me. But thereby I entered differently into their dance.

Through my joy and liberation, however, I at times felt a slight uneasiness as though I had been a bit too rash in giving myself over to this public pleasure in which I relinquished one of my secret chambers.

Perhaps too I was frightened of changing tempo.

(Indeed, my early pages were actually presented as pages of signs, that is to say movement that had been stabilized, stopped, interrupted.)

Everyone seeks, without anyone ever having told them, to maintain their tempo. Through thick and thin. Through events, emotions, adventures, just as they must, through cold seasons, in torrid lands, keep a steady temperature.

By a highly skillful[1] and constant balance between impulses that one accepts and impulses on which one turns one's back, by a complex equilibrium in which the slightest loss of speed and the slightest acceleration are ingeniously neutralized.

It is enough lightly to touch a particular spot in the hypothalamus dramatically to speed up a person's tempo, and the subject will, without being at all predisposed, through the uncontrollable acceleration of his thoughts, impressions, images, words, and many of his mental functions, be as though mad and show all the signs of manic psychosis.

Fear, prolonged anxiety, hormone changes may also bring about this change.

I was myself to discover what an awful, convulsive experience it is to change one's tempo, to lose it suddenly,[2] to find another in its place, an unknown, terribly fast tempo that one does not know how to handle, that makes everything different, unrecognizable, insane, that causes everything to overshoot itself and flash by, that cannot be followed, that must be followed, where thoughts and feelings now proceed like projectiles, where inner images as much accentuated as accelerated, bore and drill with violent, unbearable insistence, objects of an inner vision from which it is no longer possible to detach oneself, luminous like burning magnesium, agitated by a to-and-fro movement like the slide of a machine tool, infinitesimal, and which vibrate, shudder, and zig-zag, caught up in an incessant Brownian movement, images where the straight lines invested with an upward momentum are naturally vertical, cathedral lines, that have no upper limit but go on mounting indefinitely, where the broken lines in a continual seism crack, divide, crumble, and shred, where the curved lines get lost in extravagant loops, twists, and twirls, infinitely intricate lacework patternings, where objects seem set in tiny, dazzling troughs of boiling iron, where parallel lines and parallel objects indefinitely repeated and all the more forcefully the more one observes it, shatter the mind of him who vainly wishes to get back to himself in the general pullulation.

Images marked by streaming, sparkling, extreme seething, in which all remains ambiguous and, although glaringly evident, escapes being determined once and for all, and in which, although the frolics remain circumscribed within the visual field, one knows that one is under the sway of berserk trills, piercing whistles, grotesque cacophonies, and scales run amok and as though berserk.

Torn from one's tempo, in the storm of infinitesimal frenzied waves, or in the hell of equally sudden, spasmodic, and insane impulses, one can not imagine the inhuman speed ever ceasing ...

1. It might be a good idea for everyone to observe it to know how, for their part, they manage.
2. Through the action of mescaline and lysergic acid.

CATALOGUE

Untitled, 1925
COLLECTION OF CLAUDE BERRI, PARIS

Alphabet, recto, 1927

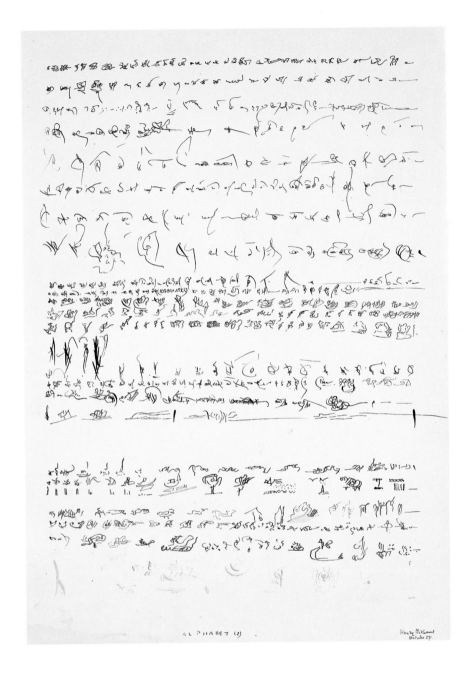

Alphabet, verso, 1927

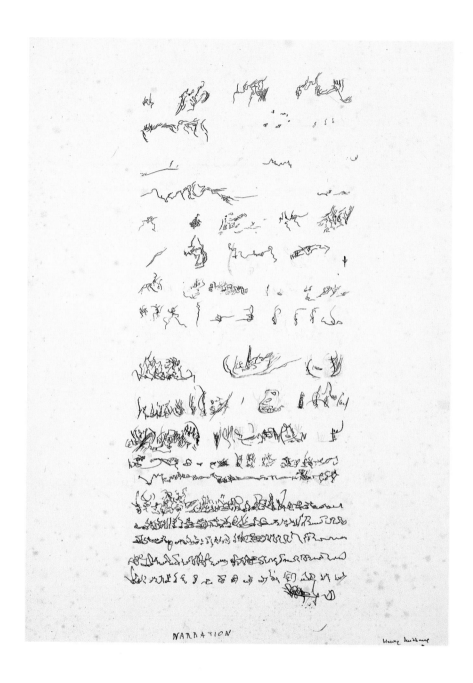

Narration, 1927
Private collection

[from *Passages*]

THE TRANSFER OF CREATIVE ACTIVITIES is one of the strangest of all voyages into the self. Strange decongestion, putting to sleep one part of the mind, the speaking, writing part (part, no rather a system of connections). You change clearing stations when you start painting.
The word-factory (thought-words, picture-words, emotion-words, motor-words) disappears, is simply, dizzyingly drowned. It no longer exists. The sprouting stops. Night. Localized death. No more desire, no: more appetite, for talking. The part of the head that used to be the most concerned with it cools off. It's a surprising experience.

And how restful!

A strange feeling. You locate the world through another window. Like a child, you have to learn to walk. You don't know a thing. You're buzzing with questions. You constantly try to guess … to plan ahead …

New problems. New temptations.

Untitled (Tropical Tree [Arbre des tropiques]), 1937

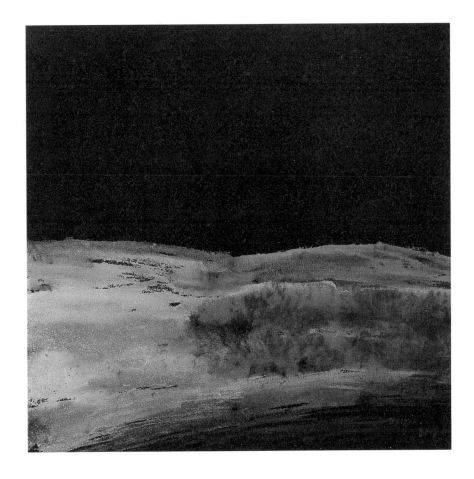

Untitled, 1938–39
COLLECTION OF CLAUDE BERRI, PARIS

Untitled (*The Blue Ladder* [*L'Échelle bleue*]), 1938
COLLECTION OF MAURICE IMBERT, PARIS

Untitled (Lying Down [Couché]), 1938

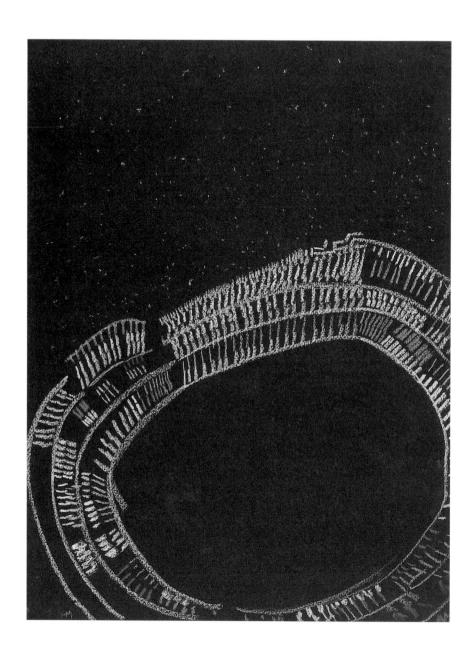

The Arena [L'Arène], 1938
MUSÉE NATIONAL D'ART MODERNE, CENTRE GEORGES POMPIDOU, PARIS

[From *Passages*]

THE FLASHING BY OF COLORS LIKE FISHES on the expanse of water where I put them, that's what I like about watercolors.

The little heap of color that breaks down into tiny particles, these trails and not the final halt, the picture. In a word, what I appreciate most in painting is cinema.

Paper that soaks up, madly, in vast quantities, persistently, deeply, this is what means more to me than colors, which in any case I merely put down as bait, as detectors, as masses to be ungorged.

Most often, most naturally, I use red. What is spilt more easily than blood? ...

Water of watercolors, as immense as a lake, water, omnivore-demon, carrying away islands, creating mirages, breaking down dams, overflowing from worlds ...

I note with a secret joy that becomes increasingly evident this leakage from the line of my drawing, in the water and the all-pervading seeping.

This truancy that so closely resembles the pattern of my life, this instantaneous treachery, this letting go that becomes ever more pronounced and leaves me feeling ever more helpless, here on the contrary fascinates me and restores me to myself, through the success of this instantaneous and gradual quid pro quo, making an absurd muddle of my lines that were clearly marked out to begin with, that swim away on all sides, carrying off my subject towards a blur that unceasingly dilates, or changes tack, surface of dissolution, divergence and distortion, journeying towards a re-absurdity that leaves me gaping on the shore.

Untitled, 1942–44
COLLECTION OF MRS. EDWIN ENGELBERTS, GENEVA

Untitled, 1942–44
COLLECTION OF MRS. EDWIN ENGELBERTS, GENEVA

Untitled, 1942–44
COLLECTION OF MRS. EDWIN ENGELBERTS, GENEVA

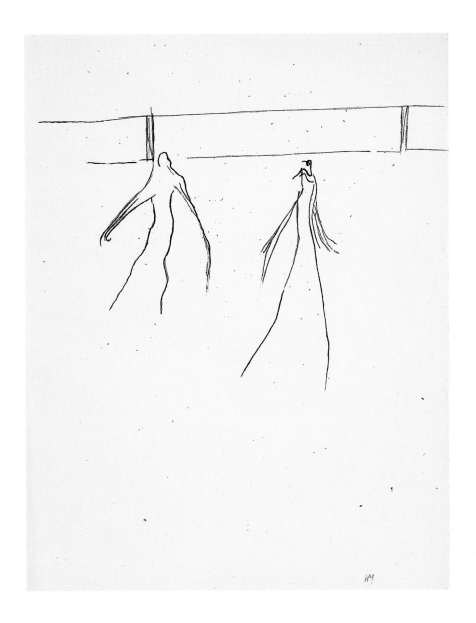

Untitled, 1944
PRIVATE COLLECTION

Untitled, 1944
COLLECTION OF MRS. EDWIN ENGELBERTS, GENEVA

Untitled, 1945–46
PRIVATE COLLECTION

Untitled, 1944
COLLECTION OF CLAUDE BERRI, PARIS

Untitled, 1951
COLLECTION OF CLAUDE BERRI, PARIS

Untitled, 1945–46

Untitled, 1945–46
Cabinet des dessins des Musées d'art et d'histoire, Geneva

Untitled, 1945–46
Private collection

Untitled, 1945–46
PRIVATE COLLECTION

Untitled (Alphabet), 1944
PRIVATE COLLECTION

Untitled (Alphabet), 1944
Cabinet des dessins des Musées d'art et d'histoire, Geneva

Untitled (Alphabet), 1944
PRIVATE COLLECTION

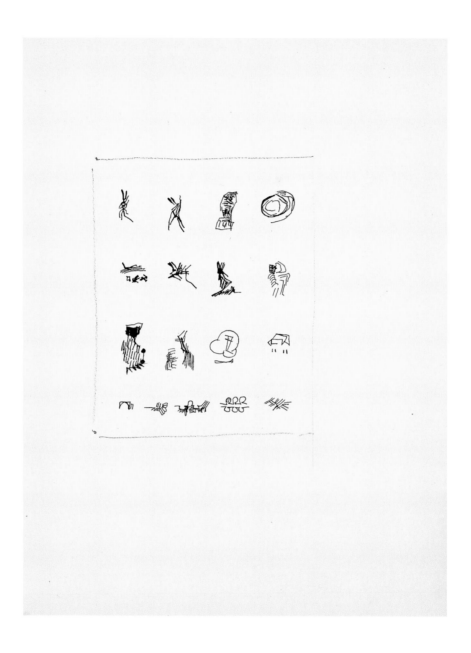

Untitled (Alphabet), 1944

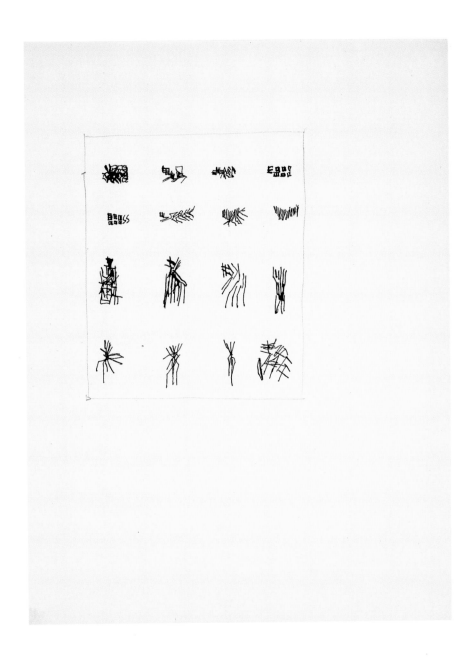

Untitled (Alphabet), 1944
PRIVATE COLLECTION

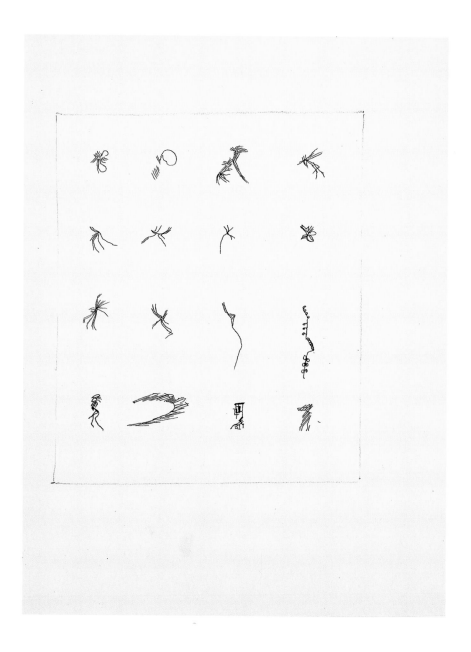

Untitled (Alphabet), 1944
CABINET DES DESSINS DES MUSÉES D'ART ET D'HISTOIRE, GENEVA

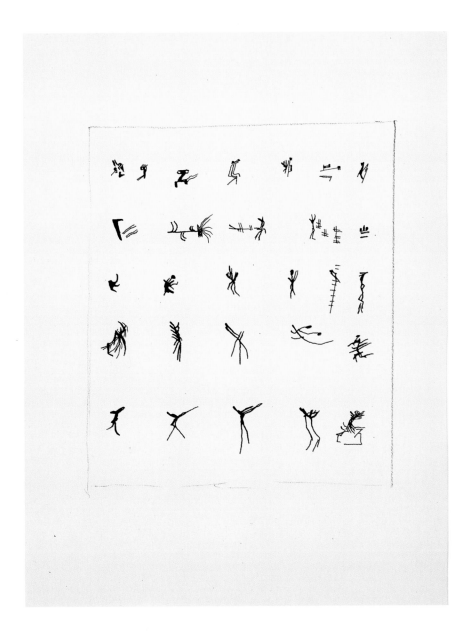

Untitled (Alphabet), 1944
PRIVATE COLLECTION

[From *Mouvements*]

SIGNS OF THE TEN THOUSAND WAYS of keeping one's balance in this moving world that
    scoffs at adaptation
signs above all to retrieve one's being from the trap of the language of others
made to get the better of you, like a well-regulated roulette wheel
granting you a few good goes
and ruin and defeat in the end
all laid down beforehand for you, as for everyone

Signs not to retrace one's steps
but to facilitate headway at every instant
signs not from copying
but by way of signs piloting
or headlong being piloted

Signs, not to be complete
but true to one's passing
signs not to conjugate
but to regain the gift of tongues
one's own at least, or else who will speak it?

Direct writing for unwinding
from the compact spool of forms
to unchoke, to revoke
to clear the billboard mind of our times of its heavy glut of images
Lacking aura, at least let's cast our effluvia to the winds.

Untitled (Movements [Mouvements]), 1950–51

Untitled (*Movements* [*Mouvements*]), 1950–51

Untitled (*Movements* [*Mouvements*]), 1950–51

Untitled (*Movements* [*Mouvements*]), 1950–51

Untitled (Movements [Mouvements]), 1950–51

Untitled (*Movements* [*Mouvements*]), 1950–51
PRIVATE COLLECTION

Untitled (Movements [Mouvements]), 1950–51
PRIVATE COLLECTION

Untitled (*Movements* [*Mouvements*]), 1950–51

Untitled (*Movements* [*Mouvements*]), 1950–51

Untitled (*Movements* [*Mouvements*]), 1950–51
Cabinet des dessins des Musées d'art et d'histoire, Geneva

Untitled (*Movements* [*Mouvements*]), 1950–51

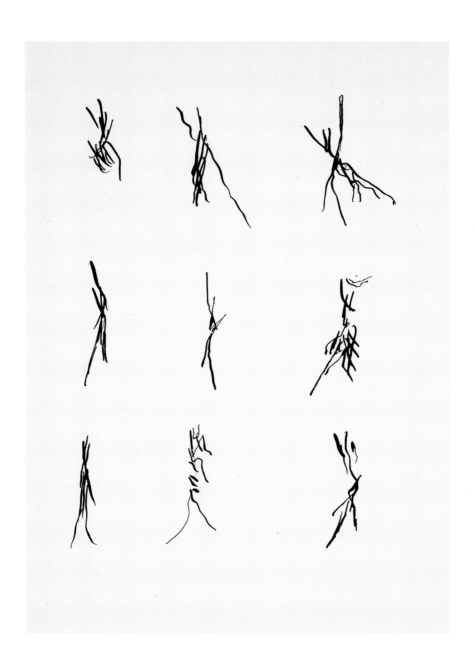

Untitled (*Movements* [*Mouvements*]), 1950–51

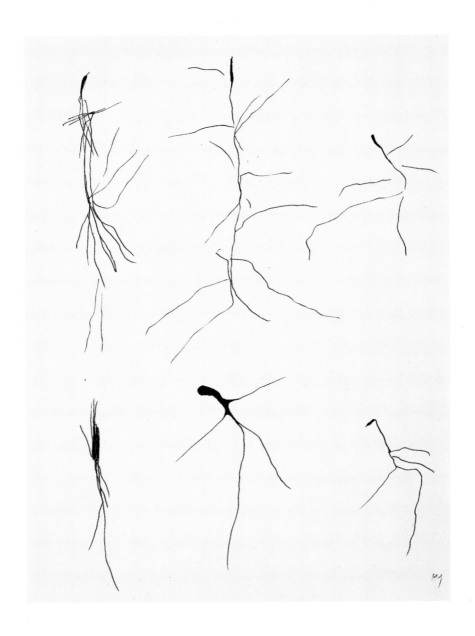

Untitled (*Movements* [*Mouvements*]), 1951
PRIVATE COLLECTION, COURTESY OF GALERIE THESSA HEROLD, PARIS

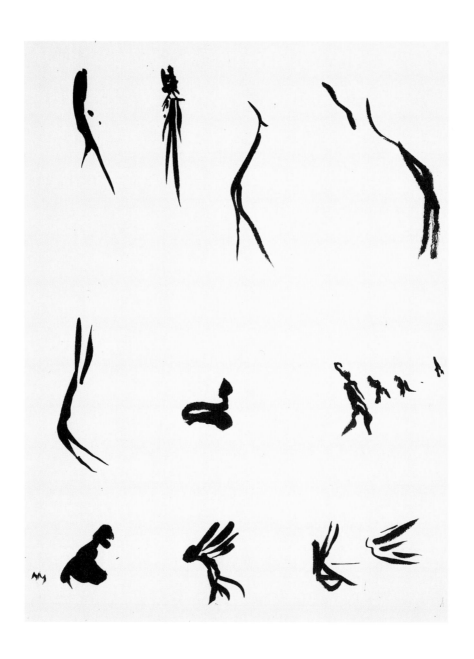

Untitled (Movements [Mouvements]), 1951
PRIVATE COLLECTION, COURTESY OF GALERIE THESSA HEROLD, PARIS

Untitled (*Movements* [*Mouvements*]), 1951
COLLECTION OF MR. AND MRS. CLAUDE FRONTISI

Untitled (*Movements* [*Mouvements*]), 1951
<small>COLLECTION OF CLAUDE BERRI, PARIS</small>

[From Postface, *Mouvements*]

THEIR MOVEMENT BECAME MY MOVEMENT. The more there were of them, the more I existed. The more of them I wanted. Creating them, I became quite other. I invaded my body (my centers of action and repose). It's often a bit remote from my head, my body. I held it now, tingling, electric. Like a rider on a galloping horse that together make but one. I was possessed by movements, on edge with these forms that came to me rhythmically. Often one rhythm ruled the page, sometimes several pages in succession, and the more numerous were the signs that appeared (one day there were close on five thousand), the more alive they were.

Although this—must I say experiment? may be repeated by many, I should like to warn anyone who prizes personal explanations that I see here the reward of indolence.

The greater part of my life, stretched out on my bed for interminable hours of which I never tired, I imparted motion to one or two or three forms, but always one more quickly, more to the fore, more diabolically quickly than any other. Instead of exalting it, investing it with riches, happiness, earthly goods as they are called, I gave it, as very poor as it remained in other respects, I instilled in it a quite extraordinary mobility of which I was the counterpart and the motor, albeit unmoving and slothful. Electrified it, while I myself was the despair of active people or the object of their scorn.

All I have done here is to repeat, sort of, on paper, in Indian ink, some of the innumerable minutes of my useless life …

R.B. points out that in this book drawing and writing are not equivalent, the former being freer and the latter more dense.

There's nothing astonishing about that. They are not the same age. The drawings are quite new in me, especially these, in the very process of being born, in the state of innocence, of surprise; but the words, the words came afterwards, afterwards, always afterwards … and so many others. How could they set me free? On the contrary, it is through having freed me from words, those tenacious partners, that the drawings are frisky and almost joyous, that their movements came buoyantly to me even in exasperation. And so I see in them a new language, spurning the verbal, and so I see them as *liberators*.

Whoever, having perused my signs, is led by my example to create signs himself according to his being and his needs will, unless I am very much mistaken, discover a source of exhilaration, a release such as he has never known, a disencrustation, a new life open to him, a writing unhoped for, affording relief, in which he will be able at last to express himself far from words, words, the words of others.

Untitled, 1955
COLLECTION OF MRS. EDWIN ENGELBERTS, GENEVA

Untitled, 1958
COLLECTION OF CLAUDE BERRI, PARIS

Untitled, 1958

Untitled (The Three Suns [Les Trois Soleils]), 1958
COLLECTION OF MARIE-CLAUDE TUBIANA, PARIS

65

Untitled, 1958–59
GALERIE THESSA HEROLD, PARIS

Untitled, 1958–59
GALERIE THESSA HEROLD, PARIS

Untitled, 1959
GALERIE THESSA HEROLD, PARIS

Untitled, 1959
GALERIE THESSA HEROLD, PARIS

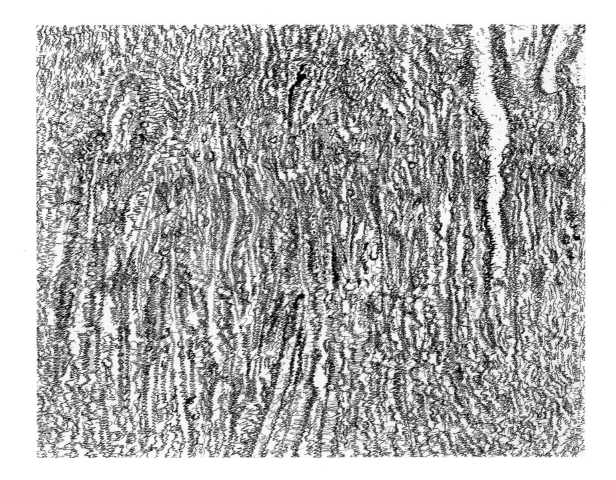

Mescaline drawing, 1955
COLLECTION OF CLAUDE BERRI, PARIS

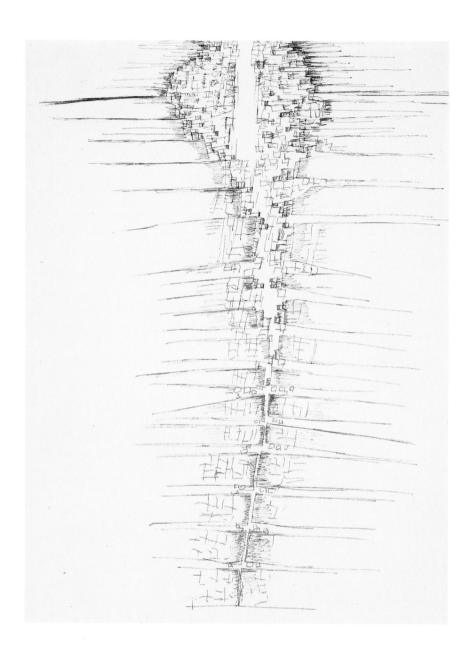

Mescaline drawing, 1955
Private collection

Psilocybin drawing, 1956

Mescaline drawing, 1956

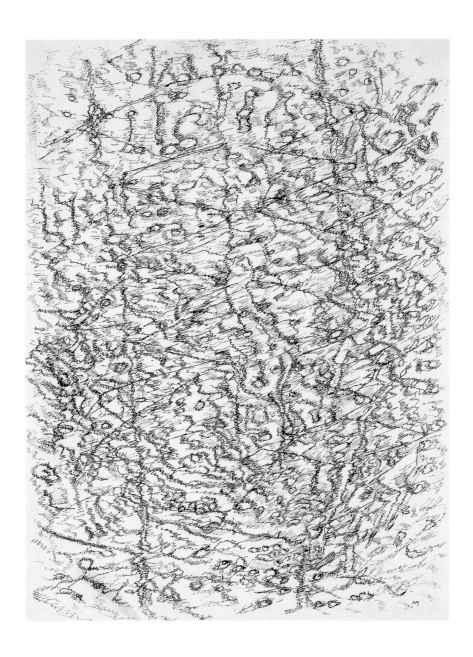

Mescaline drawing, 1956
JPC Collection, Geneva

Mescaline drawing, c. 1956

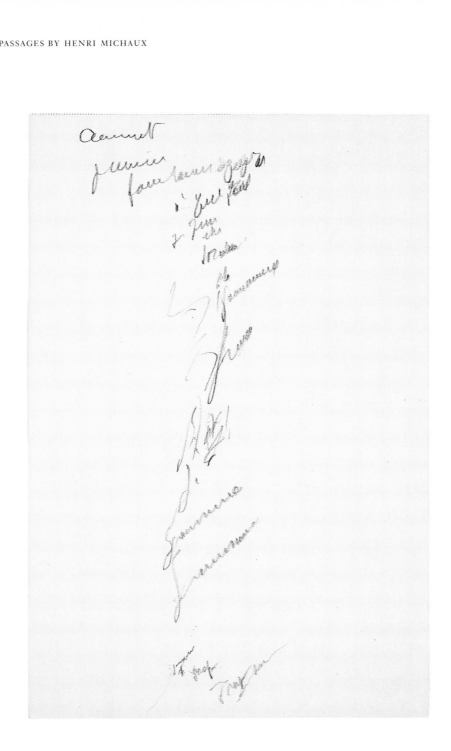

Mescaline drawing, c. 1956

Mescaline drawing, 1956–58
Private collection

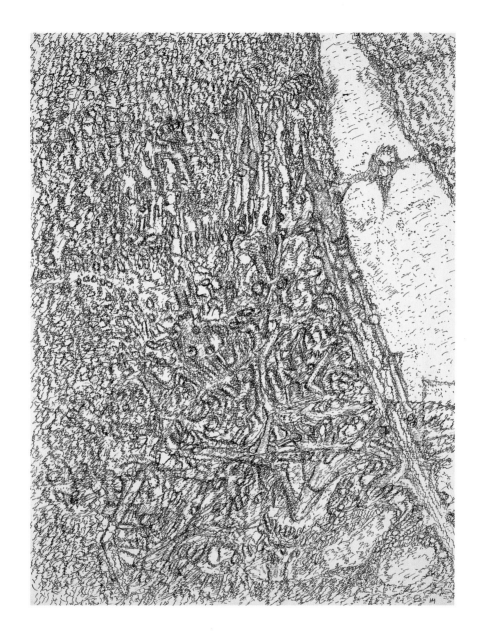

Mescaline drawing, 1958
Musée national d'art moderne, Centre Georges Pompidou, Paris

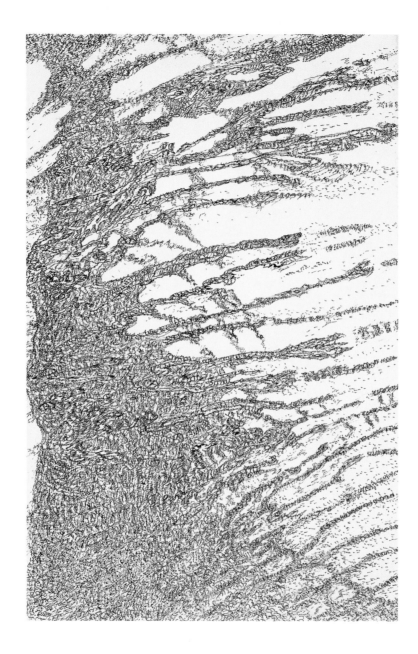

Mescaline drawing, 1957

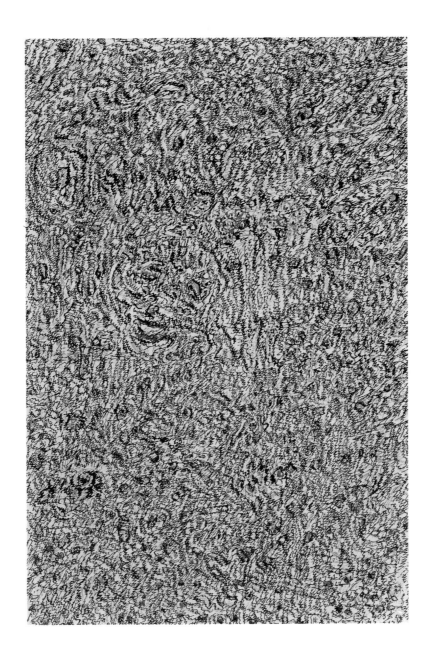

Mescaline drawing, 1959
COLLECTION OF PIERRE ALECHINSKY, BOUGIVAL, FRANCE

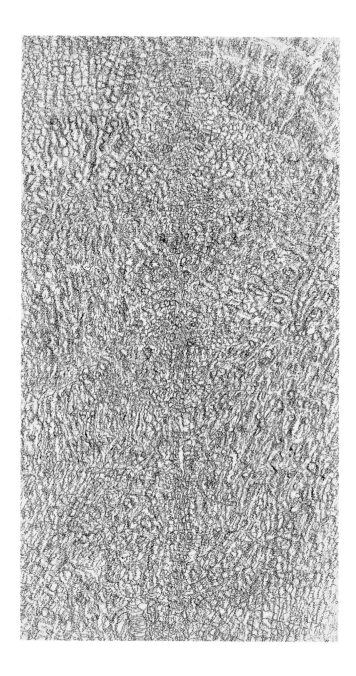

Mescaline drawing, c. 1958
COLLECTION OF CLAUDE BERRI, PARIS

Mescaline drawing, 1958–59

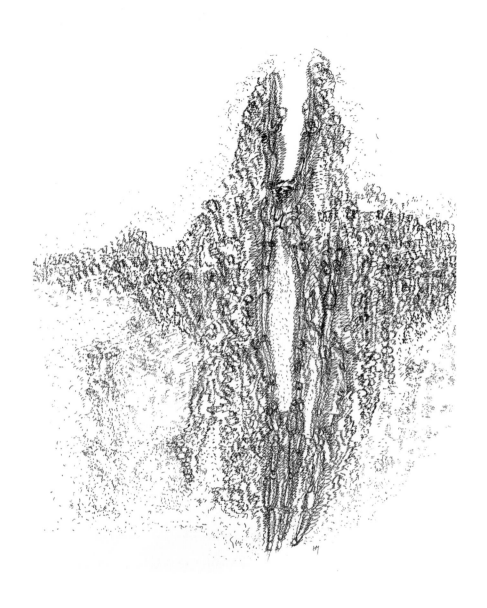

Mescaline drawing, 1960
The Museum of Modern Art, New York

[From *Paix dans les brisements*]

SO IT CAME POURING FORTH. But more violently, more electrically, more fantastically. For hours, the first ones especially, the ones most fraught with images. With my eyes closed, I watched in a vision a sort of vertical torrent come tumbling tumultuously down ...

This long, vibrantile carpet that had something in common with a discharge of electricity, sparks branching out, and that also resembled magnetic tracings, this indefinable quivering, burning, seething, like spasms for nerves, this tree with delicate branches, or with what could just as well have been outpourings along its sides, this tempestuous, contractile fluid, shaken up and frothing, ready to bubble forth but held back elastically and prevented from overflowing by a kind of surface tension, this nervous projection screen, even more mysterious than the visions that alighted there, I do not know, nor will I ever know, how to speak of it fittingly. Nothing like it is known. No one, so far as I know, has ever heard of anything that approaches it. But who can say that by virtue of some new action upon the regions of the mind, it will not one day be visible to almost anyone who wants to see it, and then that which I have drawn, singular till now, will be recognized.

Meanwhile it bubbled, before me, for me, through me, a furious and impetuous seething, and I myself was part of the seething, caught up in the onward movement, onward into the onward, in the violent haste, the squalls, the wrenchings, maddened, confounded particularly in the face of these passages of me revealed on the unexpected and incredibly luminous small screen, in a total silence, a baffling silence ...

Despite its curious and novel appearance, I believe that I am showing a basic phenomenon that was bound to be discovered one day. Here it was glaring and unconcealed, here it was exceptional in a state of exception, but—unless I am very much mistaken—it is a primeval and general phenomenon that underlies even the most placid consciousness, the most strictly controlled and headstrong intelligence, and that, perhaps vaguely felt, but not seen, passes by unperceived behind other perceptions that are of greater interest.

I believe then, that I am showing, having several times for many hours been in its then-prodigious presence, I believe that I am showing the tree without end, the tree of life that is a source, that is, dotted with words and images and propounding riddles, the flow that, without interruption, even for one single second, passes through man from the very first moment of his life right up to the last, stream or sandglass, that only stops when life stops ...

The present drawings are, need I say? reconstructions. A hand two hundred times more agile than the human hand would not be up to the task of following the speeding course of the inexhaustible spectacle.

And it is out of the question to do anything other than follow. It is not possible here to take hold of thoughts, words, or forms, in order to elaborate on them, draw inspiration from them or improvise them. All power over them has been lost. Such is the price of their speed, their independence.

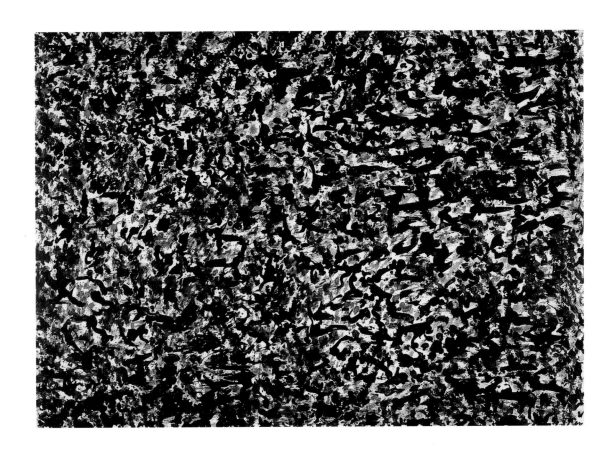

Untitled, 1959
PRIVATE COLLECTION

Untitled, 1959

88

Untitled, 1960
FONDATION MAEGHT, SAINT-PAUL-DE-VENCE, FRANCE

Untitled, 1960
THE MUSEUM OF MODERN ART, NEW YORK

Untitled, c. 1960
Musée national d'art moderne, Centre Georges Pompidou, Paris

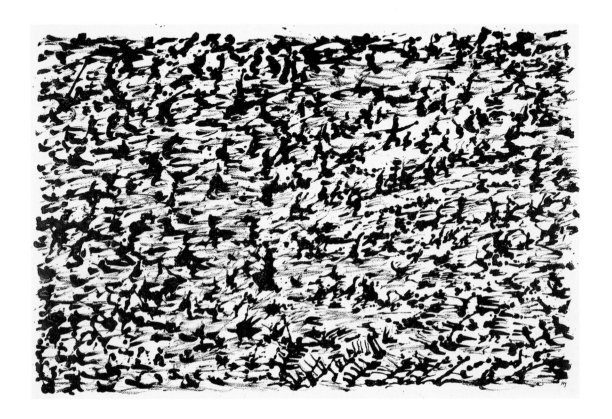

Untitled, 1960

Untitled, 1960
PRIVATE COLLECTION

93

Untitled, 1960
<small>PRIVATE COLLECTION</small>

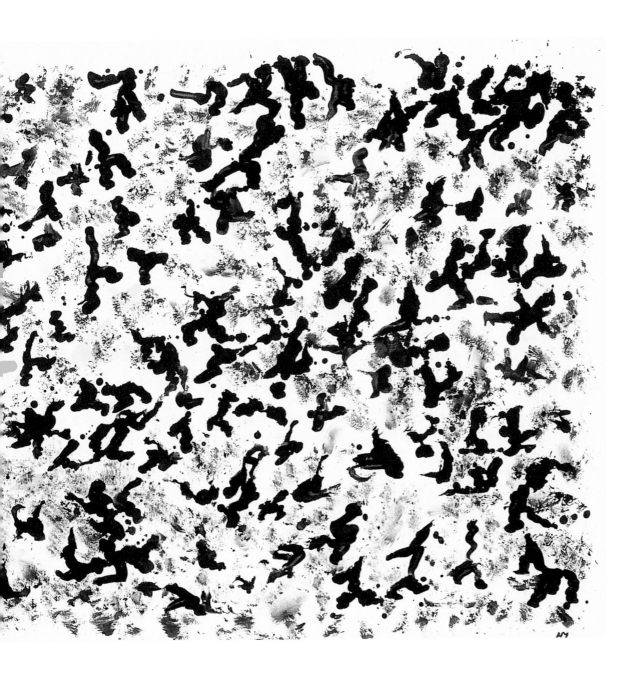

Untitled, 1961
COLLECTION OF CLAUDE BERRI, PARIS

Untitled, 1961
PRIVATE COLLECTION, COURTESY OF GALERIE THESSA HEROLD, PARIS

Untitled, 1961

Untitled (*Painting in Indian ink* [*Peinture à l'encre de Chine*]), 1962
MUSÉE NATIONAL D'ART MODERNE, CENTRE GEORGES POMPIDOU, PARIS

Untitled (*Painting in Indian ink* [*Peinture à l'encre de Chine*]), 1962

Untitled (Painting in Indian ink [Peinture à l'encre de Chine]), 1962

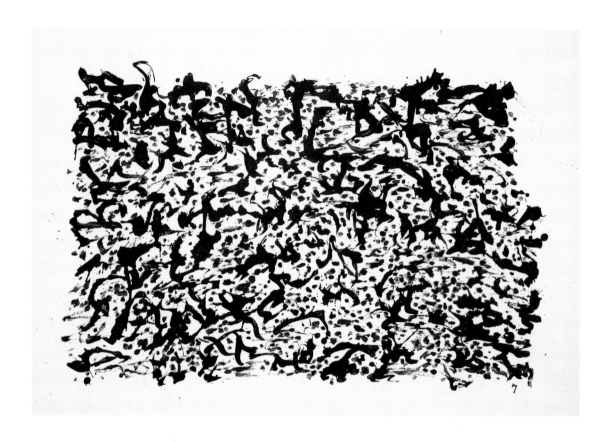

Untitled, 1961
IVAM, Institut Valencià d'Art Modern, Spain

[From *Henri Michaux*]

IS A STATEMENT REALLY NECESSARY? Isn't it obvious that I paint so as to leave words behind, to put an end to the irritating question of how and why? Could it really be that I draw because I see so clearly this thing or that thing? Not at all. Quite the contrary. I do it to be perplexed again. And I am delighted if there are traps. I look for surprises. To know always would bore me. It would upset me. Must I at least be aware of what's been going on? Not even. Others will see it in another way and will perhaps be better placed to do so. Do I have a purpose? It doesn't matter. It is not what I want that must happen to me, but what tries to happen in spite of me … and happens incompletely, which is not serious. Once the work were finished I should be afraid that it might finish me too and bury me. Watch out for that. I try to rouse that which is not absolutely static within me and which may thus (who knows?) break out suddenly, a suddenly new and living movement. It is this movement that I insist must take place, this improvised spontaneous movement. I should like to paint the inner ferment, not just paint with it or thanks to it …

Now about the blots. I have said too much already. I bet that's what they are waiting for, the blots. Well, I hate them. I love the water, but them—no. They disgust me. I am never rid of them until I have made them jump, run, climb, clamber down again. In themselves they are abhorrent to me and really only blots, which tell me nothing. (I have never been able to see anything at all in a 'Rorschach Test.') So I fight them, whip them, I should like to be done at once with their prostrate stupidity, galvanize them, bewilder them, exasperate them, ally them monstrously with everything that moves in the unnameable crowd of beings, of non-beings with a rage for being, to everything, insatiable desires or knots of force, which are destined never to take form, here or elsewhere. With their troop I busy myself with curing the blots. The blots are a provocation. I meet it. Quickly. One must act quickly with those big limp ones that are apt to go wallowing everywhere. The crucial minute comes quickly. Quickly, before they extend their realm of abjectness and vomiting. Unbearable blots. If I'm a 'tachiste,' I'm one who can't stand '*taches*' [blots].

Untitled, 1961–62

Untitled, 1961
PRIVATE COLLECTION

Untitled, 1961
COLLECTION OF CLAUDE BERRI, PARIS

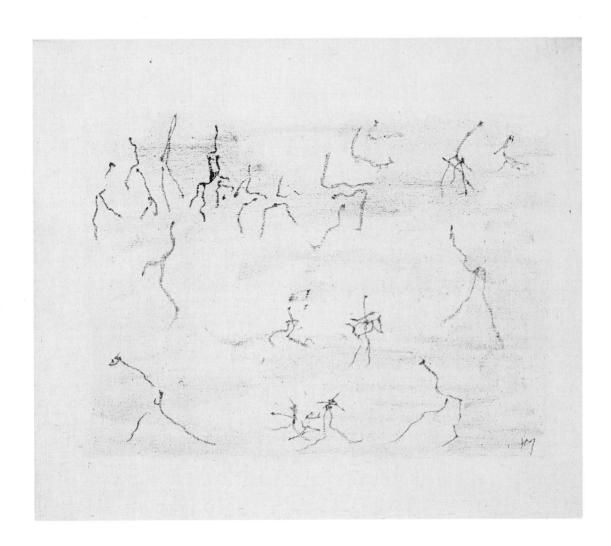

Untitled, 1961

Untitled, 1961
Musée national d'art moderne, Centre Georges Pompidou, Paris

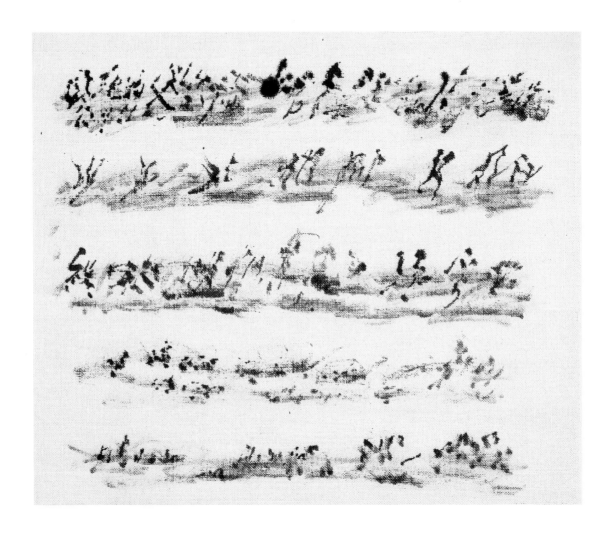

Untitled, 1961

Untitled, c. 1961

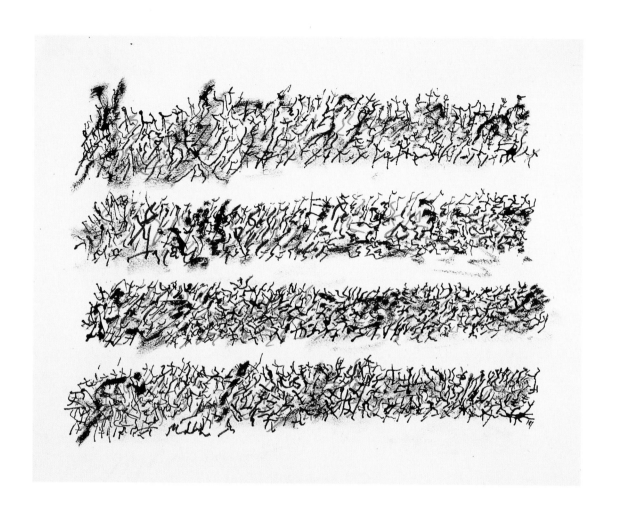

Untitled, 1962

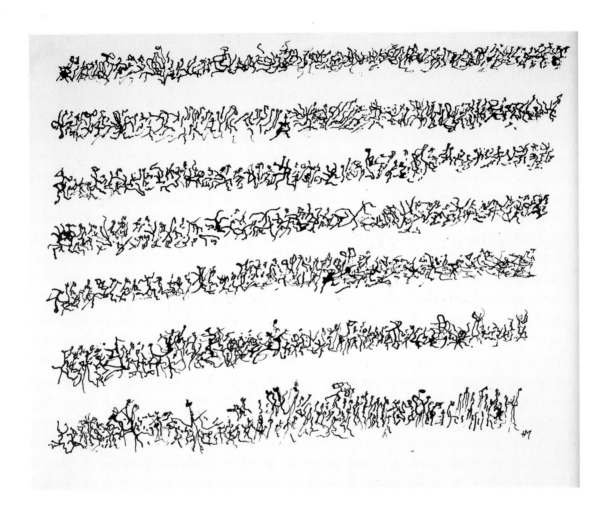

Untitled (*Painting in Indian ink* [*Peinture à l'encre de Chine*]), 1962
MUSÉE NATIONAL D'ART MODERNE, CENTRE GEORGES POMPIDOU, PARIS

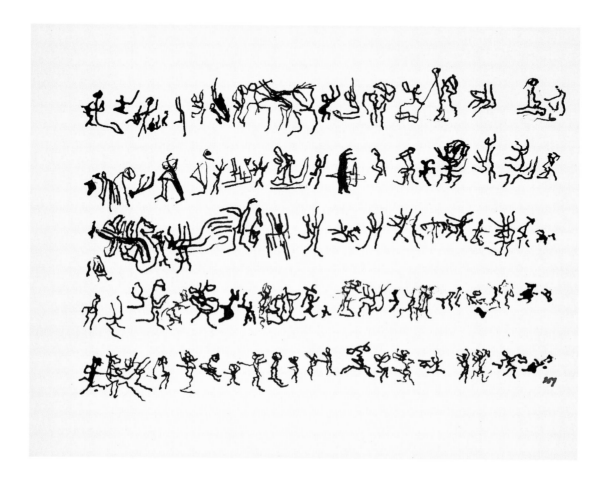

Untitled, 1963
PRIVATE COLLECTION

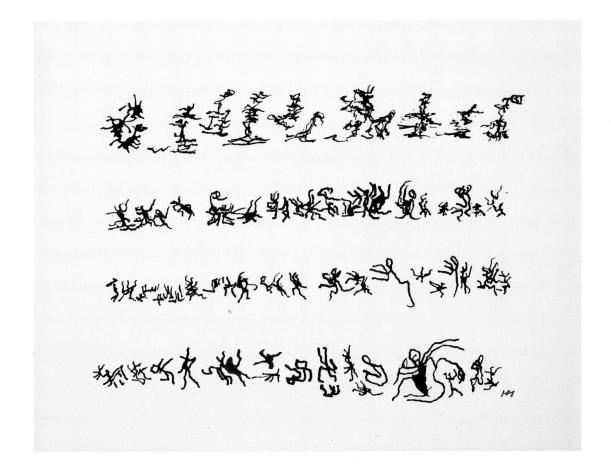

Untitled, 1966
COLLECTION OF CLAUDE BERRI, PARIS

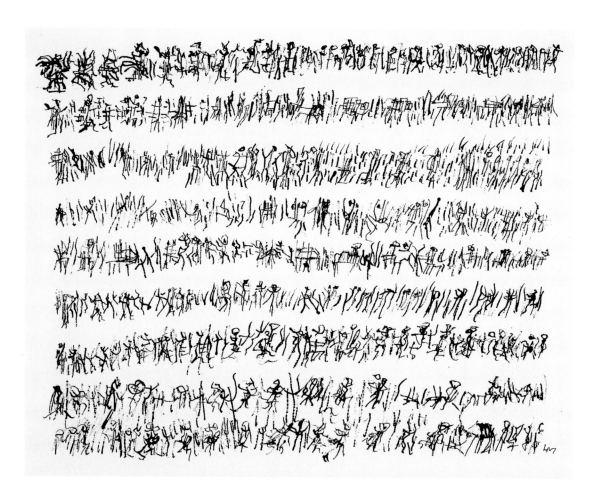

Untitled, 1963

Untitled, 1962–63
COLLECTION OF CLAUDE BERRI, PARIS

Mescaline drawing, n.d.
COLLECTION OF MARIE-CLAUDE TUBIANA, PARIS

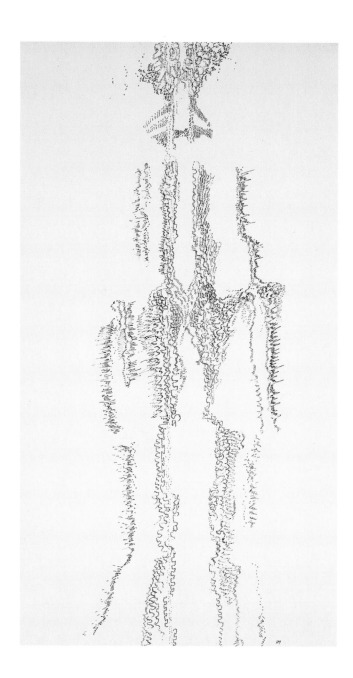

Mescaline drawing, n.d.
PRIVATE COLLECTION

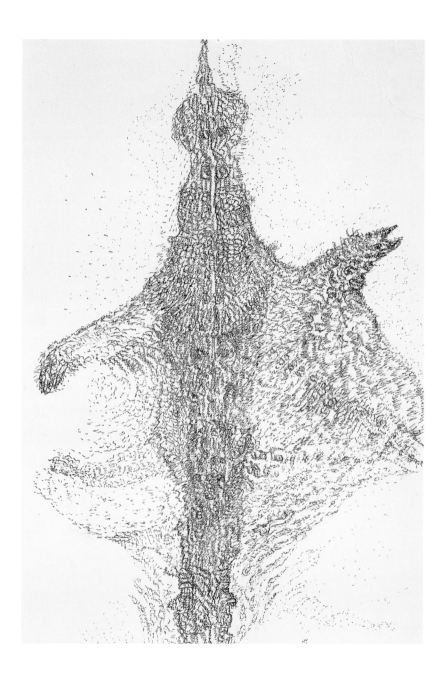

Mescaline drawing, n.d.

Inner Branchings [*Arborescences intérieures*], *c.* 1962–64
Musée national d'art moderne, Centre Georges Pompidou, Paris

Post-mescaline drawing, 1965
JPC Collection, Geneva

Post-mescaline drawing, 1966
IVAM, Institut Valencià d'Art Modern, Spain

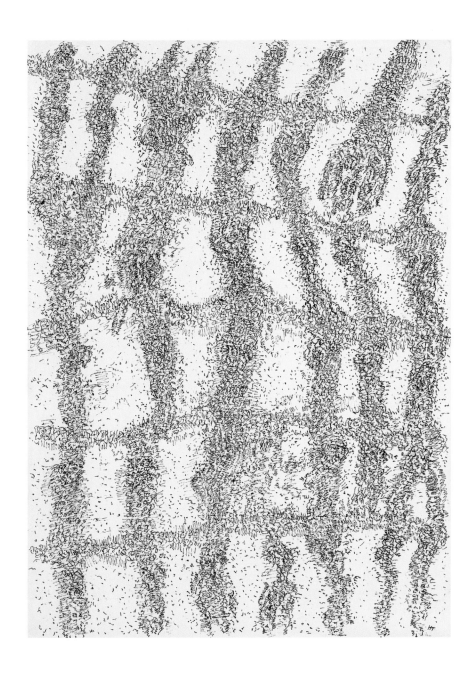

Post-mescaline drawing, 1966
COLLECTION OF CLAUDE BERRI, PARIS

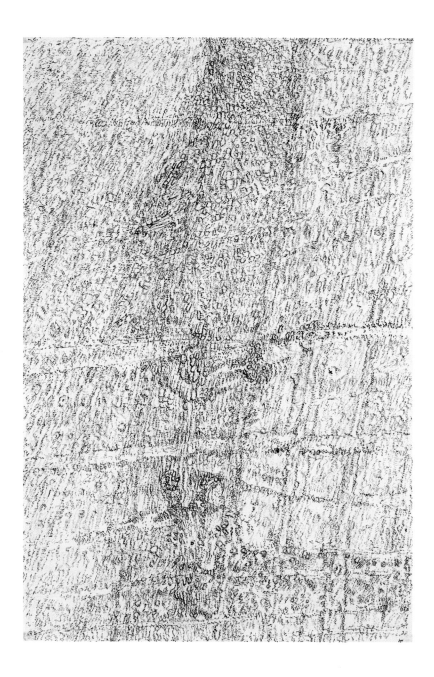

Post-mescaline drawing, 1966
Musée de Valence, France

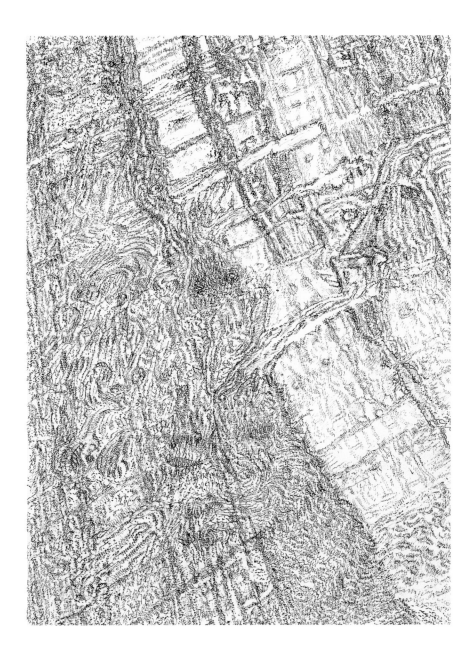

Post-mescaline drawing, c. 1969

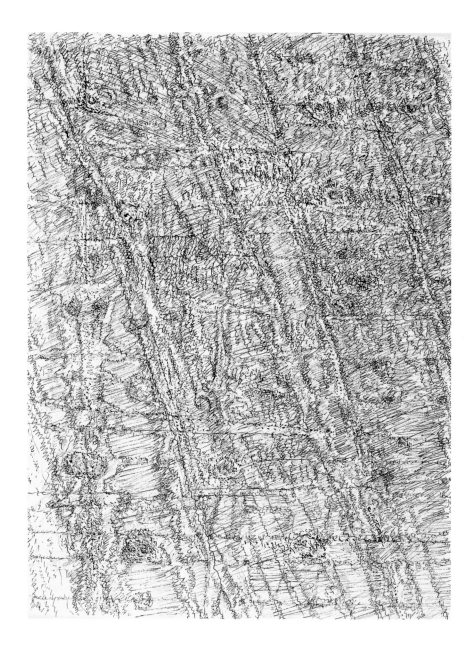

Post-mescaline drawing, c. 1969
Private collection

[From *Henri Michaux*]

MESCALINE DRAWINGS. About these, yes, I ought to make a statement (again …). They do in fact happen differently. Strange, strange experience of mescaline, stranger than any drawing could be, even if it were to cover a whole wall with its pointed lines. When one first becomes conscious of internal images (and of external phenomena as well), it is only with a certain limited quantity of consciousness, a certain restricted speed of consciousness succeeding each other and making 'contact.'

Mescaline multiplies, sharpens, accelerates, intensifies the inner moments of becoming conscious. You watch their extraordinary flood, mesmerized, uncomprehending. With your eyes shut, you are in the presence of an immense world. Nothing has prepared you for this. You don't recognize it. Tremendously present, active, colored, swarming in tiny islands very close together with no empty space, teeming, vibrating but stationary, festering with ornaments, saturating the space that still remains immeasurable, that keeps coming to life in seethings, twistings, intertwinings, in unpreventable accumulations …

That world is another consciousness …

Temples of monotonous contemplation, with ornaments and columns endlessly repeated by the novices of the perpetual … Temples of indigent infinity, revealed incessantly, without progress, in a senile, mechanical serenity, devoid of life (of this life) or the eruptions and grimaces of the great Terrifier with his unheard-of rhythms. Each one unknowingly adds his uneasiness, his banality; simple, uneducated people contribute their poor riches. A strange world, that other one, where each sees in a different way, where only the mad multiplication, the accumulation, the repetition have been perceived by everyone.

As for myself, I have usually (not always) seen the rhythms, the counter-rhythms. Much remains for me to do. I need other materials and another technique (especially for the colors). I had first of all to record the rhythms accurately, and the process of infinitization through the infinitesimal … I am just beginning.

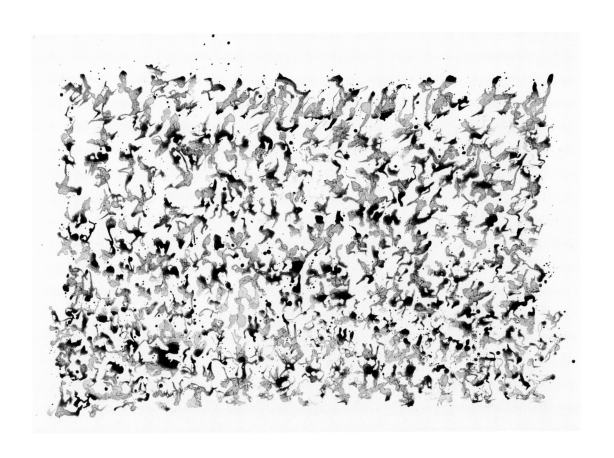

Untitled, 1968

Untitled, 1968
FONDATION MAEGHT, SAINT-PAUL-DE-VENCE, FRANCE

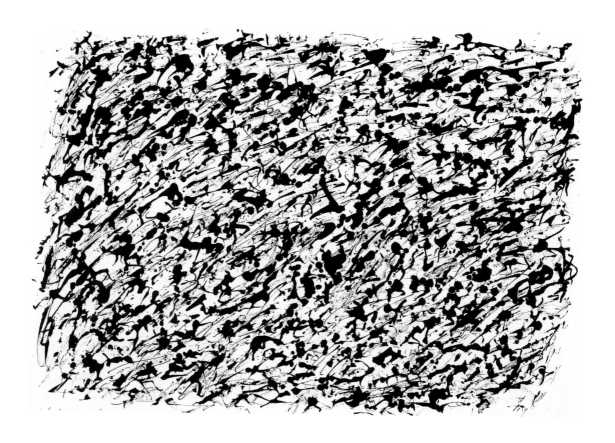

Untitled, 1970
GALERIE THESSA HEROLD, PARIS

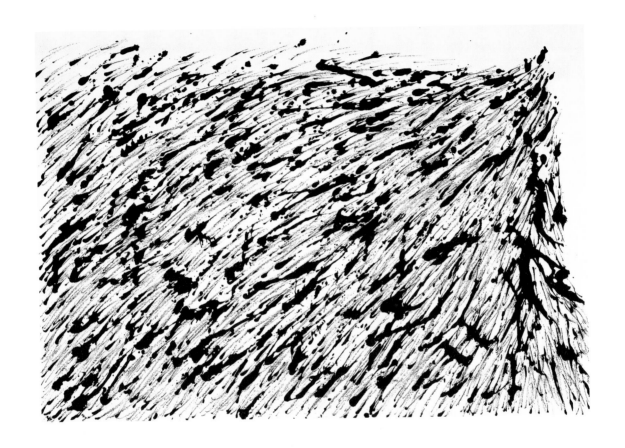

Untitled, c. 1970

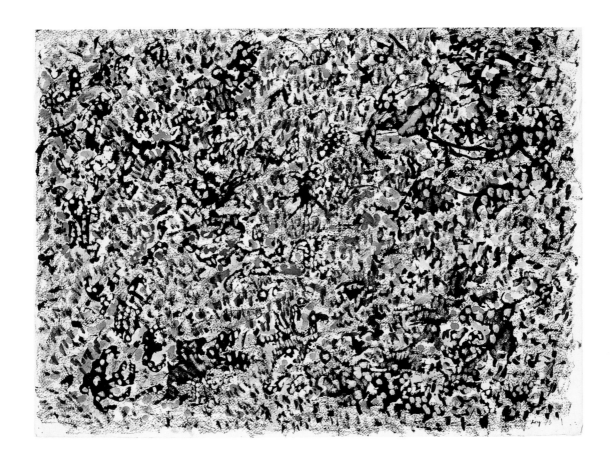

Untitled, 1973
PRIVATE COLLECTION

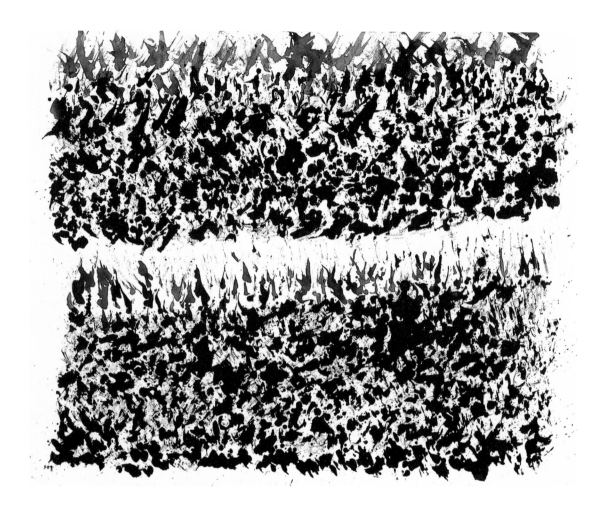

Untitled, 1968
COLLECTION OF CATHERINE PUTMAN, PARIS

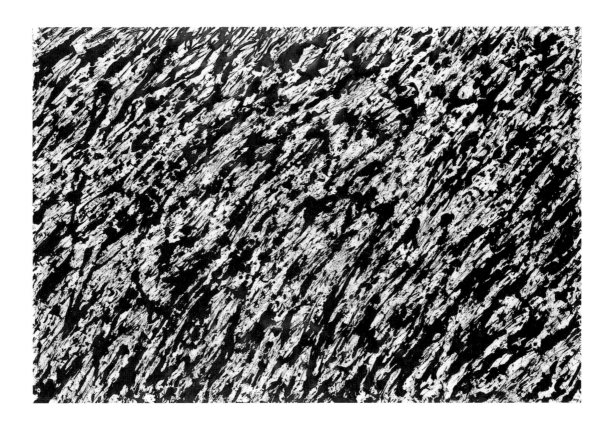

Untitled, 1976
JPC Collection, Geneva

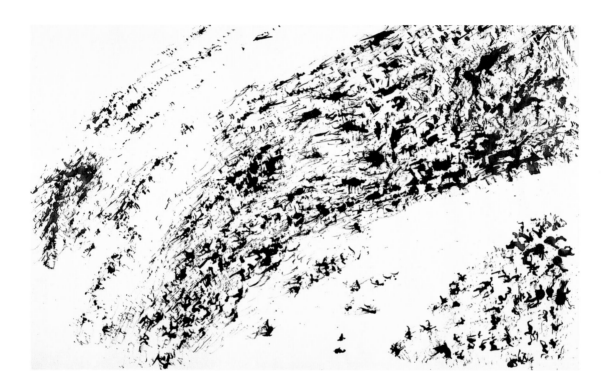

Untitled, c. 1975
PRIVATE COLLECTION

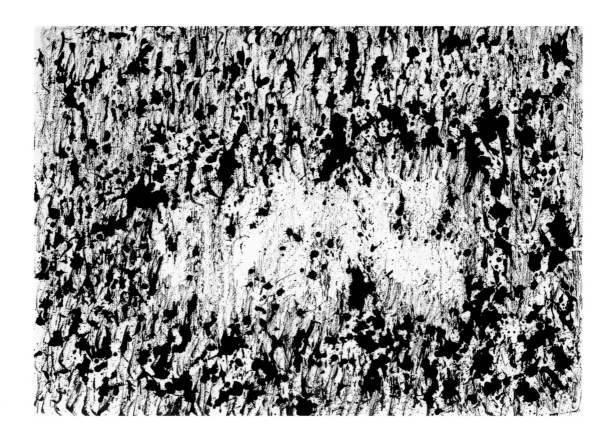

Untitled (*Cave* [*Caverne*]), n.d.

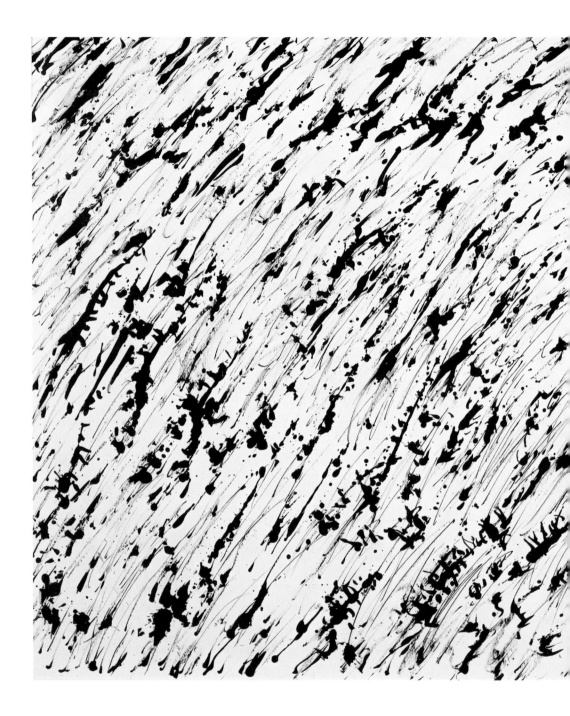

Untitled, 1975
PRIVATE COLLECTION

Untitled (By Way of Rhythms [Par la voie des rythmes]), 1974

Untitled (*By Way of Rhythms* [*Par la voie des rythmes*]), 1974

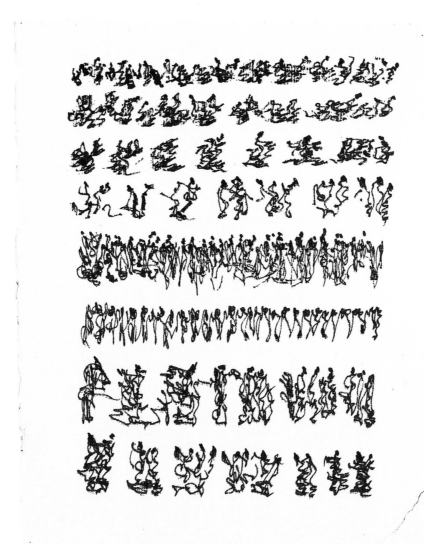

Untitled (*By Way of Rhythms* [*Par la voie des rythmes*]), 1974
PRIVATE COLLECTION

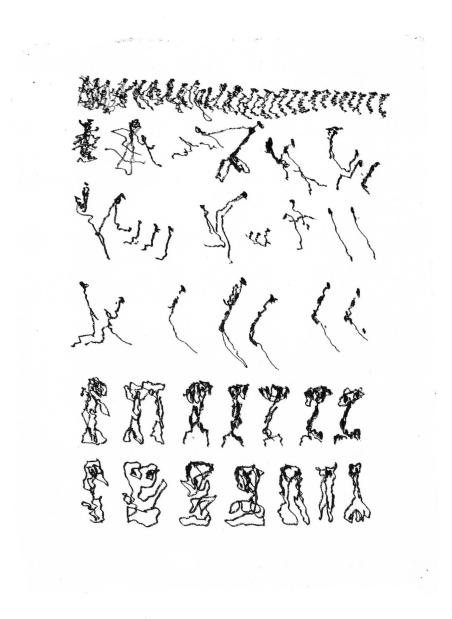

Untitled (By Way of Rhythms [Par la voie des rythmes]), 1974
PRIVATE COLLECTION

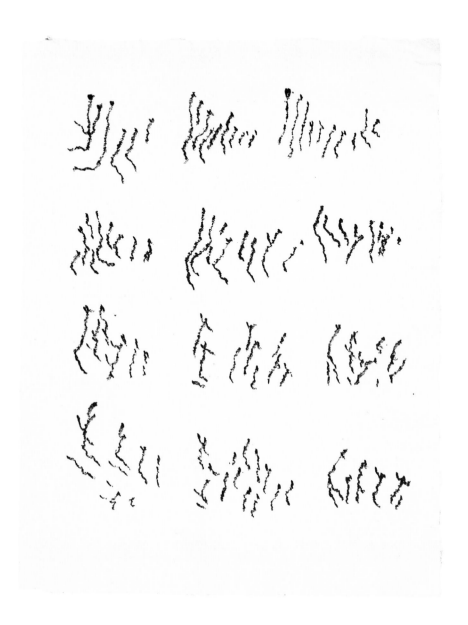

Untitled (By Way of Rhythms [Par la voie des rythmes]), 1974
PRIVATE COLLECTION

Untitled (By Way of Rhythms [Par la voie des rythmes]), 1974
PRIVATE COLLECTION

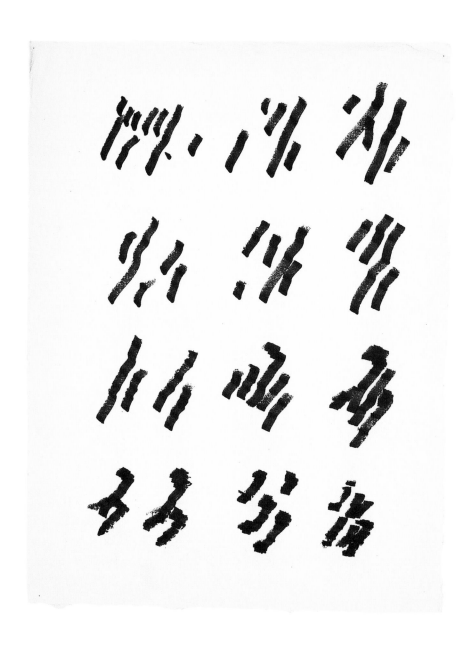

Untitled (By Way of Rhythms [Par la voie des rythmes]), 1974

Untitled (By Way of Rhythms [Par la voie des rythmes]), 1974
PRIVATE COLLECTION

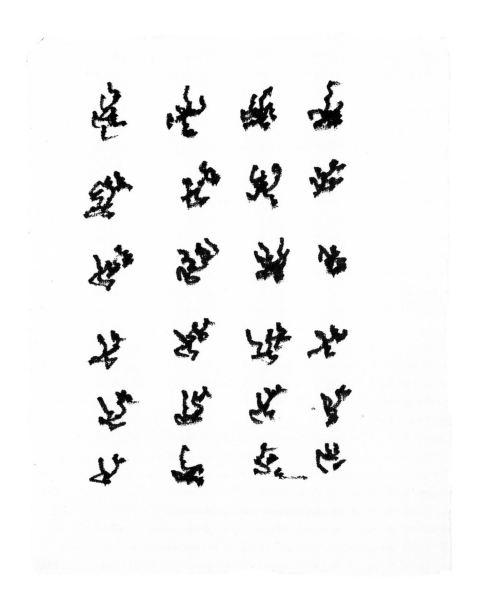

Untitled (By Way of Rhythms [Par la voie des rythmes]), 1974

Untitled (By Way of Rhythms [Par la voie des rythmes]), 1974
<small>PRIVATE COLLECTION</small>

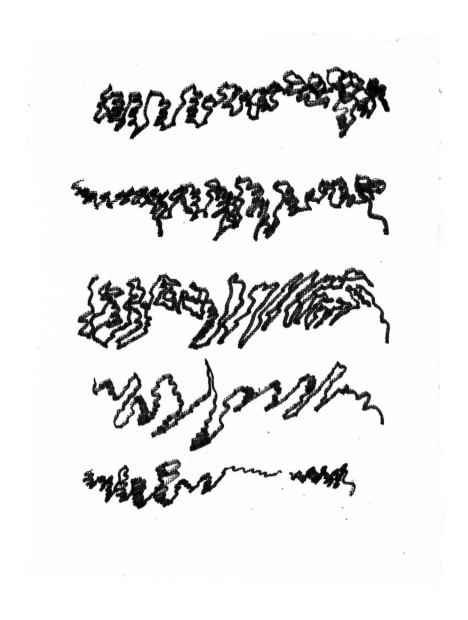

Untitled (By Way of Rhythms [Par la voie des rythmes]), 1974

Untitled (By Way of Rhythms [Par la voie des rythmes]), 1974
Private collection

Untitled, c. 1970

Untitled, 1974
PRIVATE COLLECTION

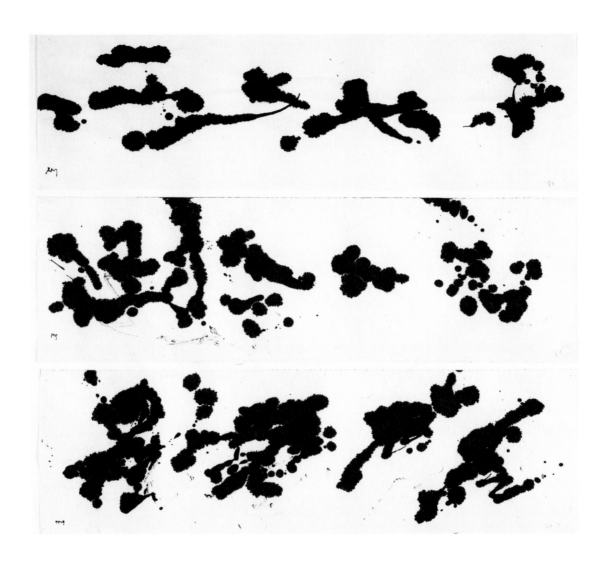

Untitled, 1980

Untitled, 1981
PRIVATE COLLECTION

Untitled (Procession of Monks, or Rather of Mandarins [*Défilé de moines ou bien de mandarins*]), 1977

[From *Ailleurs*]

The author has often lived elsewhere: two years in Garaband, about the same in the Land of Magic, a bit less in Poddema. Or a lot more. There are no precise dates.

He did not always particularly like these countries. Here and there, he nearly got used to them. Not really. When it comes to countries, the more one distrusts them the better.

He came back home after each trip. His resistance isn't infinite.

Some readers have found these countries a bit strange. That won't last. The impression is already fading.

He who sought to escape the World becomes its translator, too. Who can escape? The container is closed.

You'll see: these countries are perfectly natural after all. Soon they will be encountered everywhere … Natural as plants, insects, natural as hunger, habit, age, custom, customs, as the presence of the unknown bordering on the known. Behind that which is, which nearly was, which tended to be, threatened to be, and which among millions of 'possibilities' began to be, but was unable to settle in completely …

AN INTERVIEW WITH HENRI MICHAUX

John Ashbery

HENRI MICHAUX IS HARDLY A PAINTER, hardly even a writer, but a conscience—the most sensitive substance yet discovered for registering the fluctuating anguish of day-to-day, minute-to-minute living.

Michaux lives in Paris on the rue Séguier, in the heart of a small district of crumbling but still aristocratic palaces that seems strangely hushed and dull in spite of the proximity of St. Germain-des-Prés and the Latin Quarter. A wooden scaffolding has been put up in the stairway of the seventeenth-century *hôtel particulier* where he lives, to keep the stairs from collapsing. Michaux's apartment seems to have been carved out of a larger one. In spite of the character of the architecture and some beautiful old furniture, the effect is neutral. The walls are no-color, even the garden outside looks ghostly. Almost no pictures—a Zao Wou-ki and a Chinese painting of a horse more or less happen to be there: "Don't draw any conclusion from them." The only remarkable object is a large, brand-new radio: like many poets, many painters, Michaux prefers music.

He detests interviews, and seemed unable to remember why he had consented to this one. "But you may as well begin, since you're here." He sat with his back to the light so that it was difficult to see him; he shielded his face with his hand and contemplated me warily out of the corner of his eye. Michaux will not be photographed, and refuses to allow even a drawing of himself to be reproduced. Faces have a horrible fascination for him. He has written: "A man and his face, it's a little as if they were constantly devouring each other." To an editor who once wrote asking him for a photograph to publish in a catalogue with others, he replied: "I write in order to reveal a person whose existence no one would ever have suspected from looking at me"—this statement was published in the space that had been intended for his portrait.

Yet Michaux's face is pleasant and gentle. He is Belgian, born in Namur in 1899, and if he has the pale complexion of northern peoples, and something of their phlegm, his face can still light up in a broad Flemish grin, and he has a charming, unexpected giggle.

Has painting supplanted writing as a means of expression for him?

Not at all. In the last few years I've had three or four shows and published three or four books. Since I took up painting I do more of everything—but not at the same time. I write or paint in alternating periods.

I began painting in the mid-1930s partly as a result of a Klee show I saw, partly because of my trip to the Orient. I once asked a prostitute for directions in Osaka and she did a lovely drawing to show me. Everybody draws in the Orient.

The trip was a capital experience in Michaux's life: out of it came *Un barbare en Asie* as well as the discovery of a whole new rhythm of life and creation.

I had always thought there would be another form of expression for me—but I never thought it would be painting. But then, I'm always wrong about myself. I always wanted to be a sailor when I was young, and I tried it for a while, but I simply didn't have the physical strength necessary. I had always thought I didn't want to write, either. *C'est excellent, il faut se tromper un peu.*

Then the *cuisine* of painting annoyed me. Artists are such prima donnas—they take themselves so seriously, and they have all that *cuisine*—canvas, easel, tubes of paint. If I could, I would still prefer to be a composer. But you have to study. If there were only some way to enter directly into a keyboard ... Music hatches my dissatisfaction. My large ink drawings are already nothing but rhythm. Poetry doesn't satisfy me as much as painting—but other forms are possible.

Who are the artists who mean the most to him?

I love the work of Ernst and Klee, but they alone wouldn't have been enough to start me painting seriously. I admire the Americans less—Pollock and Tobey—but they created a climate in which I could express myself. They are instigators. They gave me *la grande permission*—yes, yes, that's very good—*la grande permission.* Just as one values the Surrealists less for what they wrote than for the permission they gave everybody to write whatever comes into their heads. And of course the Chinese classical painters showed me what could be done with just a few lines, just a few indications.

But I don't think very much about influences. You enjoy listening to people's voices in the street, but they don't solve your problem for you. When something is good it distracts you from your problem.

Did he feel that his poetry and his painting were two different forms of expression of the same thing?

Both of them try to express music. But poetry also tries to express some non-logical truth—a truth other than what you read in books. Painting is different—there is no question of truth. I make rhythms in paintings just as I would dance. This is not a *vérité.*

I asked Michaux whether he felt his experience of mescaline had had an effect on his art, other than the drawings he did under its influence, which he calls "mescalinian drawings," and which, with their hypersensitive massing of insubstantial, filament-like lines into zones, look different from the bold, abrupt work he does under normal conditions.

"Mescaline gives you more attention for everything—for details, for terribly rapid successions." Describing such an experience in his recent book, *Paix dans les brisements*, he wrote:

My trouble was great. The devastation was greater. The speed was even greater ... A hand two hundred times more agile than the human hand would not have sufficed to follow the accelerated course of that unquenchable spectacle. And there was no question of anything but following. You cannot seize a thought, a term, a figure, to work them over, get inspiration from them, improvise on them. All power is lost on them. This is the price of their speed, their independence.

He also spoke of the superhuman detachment he felt under the influence of mescaline, as though he could observe the machinery of his own mind from a distance. This detachment can be terrible, but on one occasion it resulted in a vision of beatitude, the only one in his life, which he describes in *L'Infini turbulent* : "I saw thousands of gods ... Everything was perfect ... I hadn't lived in vain ... My futile, wandering existence was at last setting foot on the miraculous road ..."

This moment of peace and fulfillment was without precedent in Michaux's experience. He hasn't sought to renew it—"It was enough that it happened." And he hasn't taken mescaline in over a year, not that he "knows." "Perhaps I'll take it again when I'm a virgin once more," he said. "But this sort of thing should be experienced only rarely. The Indians used to smoke the peace pipe only on great occasions. Today people smoke five or six packs of cigarettes a day. How can one experience anything that way?"

It had begun to grow dark in the room and the trees in the gray garden outside seemed to belong on the oozy metaphysical terrain he describes in *Mes propriétés*. I mentioned that nature appears rarely in his work. "That is not correct," he said. "At any rate, animals do. I adore animals. If ever I come to your country it will no doubt be to visit the zoos." (His only visit to America was as a sailor, in 1920, and he saw only Norfolk, Savannah, and Newport News.)

> I once had two hours to spend in Frankfurt when I had a show there, and I shocked the director of the museum by asking to see the botanical garden rather than the museum. As a matter of fact, the garden was lovely ... But since mescaline I can no longer feel a sense of fraternity with animals. The spectacle of my own mind at work somehow made me more conscious of my mind. I can no longer feel empathy with a dog, because he hasn't one. It's sad ...

We discussed the mediums he uses. Though he works with oils and watercolors, he prefers Indian ink. The large white sheets of drawing paper studded all over with hard black little knots, or strewn with vaguely human figures that suggest some hopeless battle or pilgrimage, are typical of Michaux. "With India ink I can make a small, very intense little mass," he said. "But I have other plans for ink. Among other things, I've been doing some India ink paintings on canvas. I'm enthusiastic about this, because I can be both precise and blurry with the same brush, at the same moment. It's direct; there are no risks. You're not up against the ruses of oil, the *cuisine* of painting."

In these canvases Michaux often paints three wide vertical bands, using little ink to give a dusty effect. In this vague medium swim dozens of desperately articulate little figures: birds, men, twigs, more deliberately drawn than in the drawings but animated by the same intense energy.

More than his other work, they seemed to realize his intentions for painting as he expressed them recently in the magazine *Quadrum*:

> Instead of one vision that excludes others, I would have liked to draw the moments that, placed side by side, go to make up a life. To expose the interior phrase for people to see, the phrase that has no words, a rope that uncoils sinuously, and intimately accompanies everything that impinges from the outside or the inside. I wanted to draw the consciousness of existence and the flow of time. As one takes one's pulse.

ArtNews, March 1961

Henri Michaux in his studio, photographed by Gisèle Freund, n.d.

ADVENTURES OF INK

Catherine de Zegher

Pᴇɴ ɪɴ ʜᴀɴᴅ, ᴡʀɪᴛɪɴɢ ᴏʀ ᴅʀᴀᴡɪɴɢ, forming concept or image, Henri Michaux leaves a trail of ink behind him, an invitation to the voyage.[1] A true poet and artist, he believes imagination, or rather the movement of imaginative action, to be "one of the strangest of all voyages into the self."[2] He sees himself carried away in "the poetry of incompletion preferred to eyewitness accounts, to copies. Markings launched into the air, fluttering as if caught by the motion of a sudden inspiration, and not prosaically ..."[3] It is a model of the liveliest spiritual mobility shattering the static and established images that well-defined words have become. "Born, raised, educated in an environment and culture uniquely given over to the 'verbal', I paint *to decondition myself*," Michaux opens *Émergences-Résurgences*. The non-mimetic process of his tracing becomes a way of turning the multi-dimensional experience of gestural and tactile activity into a two-dimensional experience of self-abandonment in literary space, where cultural and social underpinnings of linguistics remain both operative and under scrutiny. Taking paper and not the mirror as the site of self-observation, the interrogation of linguistic systems is Michaux's quest—and like all quests, it does not consist in discovering its object but in assuring the conditions of its impossibility.

From an early age Michaux struggled to contest many conventions of Western society, most importantly the powerful role assigned to words. As a young sailor he embarked on a worldwide journey to travel 'elsewhere,' in a spirit that was to exemplify his battle against pre-established codes. As 'a man of letters' he could be supposed to hold words in high regard, yet he was aware of how they could serve those in authority and devised numerous strategies of resistance. Marking the blank page as both a traveler and a writer, Michaux felt the limitations of words, and turned to drawing in order to attack, and to attack violently, any form of coded inertia. Beginning in the 1920s, he experimented with making his first "illegible" marks in works such as *Alphabet* and *Narration*. "Illegible writing indicates in fact that the sign has been remorsefully eaten away by its own figurative nature, and that it does indeed take almost nothing at all for the figure to resort back to its status as a mere drawing."[4] This activity allowed him to imagine an expanded linguistic system composed of not-quite-lexical but still somehow meaningful elements operating spontaneously at the junction between pictogram, line, stain, and character. Constantly in flux, his ink drawings exploded representative signs, explored the unknown, and conjured the profound and indescribable.

Whether he threw it onto paper or flung it from the pen itself, Michaux's use of ink, followed later by watercolor, was fluid, direct, and shapeless. Water-soluble, these transparent and fast-moving materials demanded the artist's absolute attentiveness, but allowed him "to draw the consciousness of existing and the flow of time. As one takes one's pulse."[5] More interested in transformation and movement than in the finished product,

Michaux loved the fluidity of the medium, its uncertainty, its freedom, and its gestural physicality. "Could it really be that I draw because I see so clearly this thing or that thing? Not at all. Quite the contrary. I do it to be perplexed again. And I am delighted if there are traps. I look for surprises."[6] In some works the starting point was a "stain," described by the artist as a "provocation" to be dealt with rapidly: "One must act quickly with those big limp ones that are apt to go wallowing everywhere. The crucial minute comes quickly. Quickly, before they extend their realm of abjectness and vomiting."[7]

Although the immediacy of his work invites comparison with the contemporaneous Surrealist practice of automatism, it was not the unconscious, but rather absolute consciousness, that Michaux sought to express. For him, writing as the reproduction of an established set of signs remained a way of making language visible and belonged to the domain of the legible. Though his writing was philosophically unsettling, his inquiry into meaning seldom involved typographical experimentation, visual prosody, or a consideration of the graphic make-up of the sign. Such fundamental disruptions within a formal level seemed to be displaced into the space of drawing. In his book *Mouvements* he developed a method of tracing vaguely suggestive inkbrush strokes "in motion" next to words in the accompanying poem, at once attacking and approving the word's status as part of a coded linguistic system that could not be ignored. Even if the structure seemed inadequate, limited, and absurd to him, it still had a sense, perhaps a *non*sense. In contrast to the Surrealists, who, through their automated experiments of free association and their abstractly formulated attempts to destroy tradition and logic, disregarded any codified, generative structure of self-expression, Michaux stayed within a pan-linguistic interdisciplinary system of expressive marks. Working from the model of Chinese ideograms, he even dreamed of a universal language of pure lines that would communicate intimately or "murmur," without forming any ideas too definitely: "Down with our swaggering languages, with their rigid, enslaving syntax and grammar! Let's have no alphabet—no words."[8] In his book *Par des traits* Michaux suggests: "The sign: finally delivering us from litanies of words, of phrases depending only on phrases, continuing in phrases, it would free the brain from its local over-occupation. … Signs that would enable us to be open to the world differently, creating and developing *a different function* in man, DISALIENATING HIM."[9]

Michaux's œuvre—where logic and a refusal of any form of logic are opposed—oscillates between order and disorder, language and non-language, form and *informe*, social utopia and personal escape; as such, its place in world literature and art is important but difficult to fix and categorize, and curiously, the work effectively achieved his purpose of researching the non-definite. John Ashbery described him as "hardly a painter, hardly even a writer, but a conscience—the most sensitive substance yet discovered for registering the fluctuating anguish of day-to-day, minute-to-minute living."[10] Some of Michaux's writings were translated into English and were venerated in the 1960s by the Californian Beat generation, in particular *Misérable miracle*, which related his experiences with mescaline. His admirers range from the poet Allen Ginsberg and the writer Jorge Luis Borges to the French rap star MC Solaar in the 1990s. Because of the resemblance in the gestural and exploratory nature of the painting and drawing, Francis Bacon, among other artists, compared Michaux to Jackson Pollock, claiming:

> I think that Michaux is a very intelligent man—intelligent and extremely well-informed—perfectly conscious of the situation in which he was implicated. It seems to me that when it comes to 'tachisme' or non-figurative signs, he is unsurpassed. I find him superior in this respect to Jackson Pollock.[11]

But then again, even if in the œuvres both of Michaux and Pollock the practice of 'action painting' and 'action drawing' seems to emerge more or less simultaneously around 1950 and connect them on a formal level, their 'performance' reveals a very different invest-igation and attempt to dissolve the object of art. Pollock's first drip painting, in 1947–48, was made in oil and bordered on the spectacular; Michaux's first 'drippings' were made in ink around 1950 and bordered on the spontaneous writing of an inner message. As Michaux's practice remains unclassifiable, it seems to escape a connection to the Abstract Expressionists as much as to the Surrealist movement.

A writer of the drawn or a drawer of the written, Michaux never abandoned pen or paper. He was the author of more than thirty books of poems, prose poems, narratives, essays, journals, and thousands of drawings. The drawings, which included a wide range of experi-ments (some of them with mescaline in the early 1940s), did not merely accompany his words, but converged and collided with them. Michaux took his writing into his drawing and his drawing into his writing, pushing the boundaries of each form of artistic practice. Letters within or without alphabets appeared as dark and powerful signs on the whiteness of the page. In "To Draw the Flow of Time" Michaux relates how, at the suggestion of a publisher, he started to enlarge characters. At the beginning, very much against his own opinion—"for can writing be enlarged?"—he seized hold of a brush (which was destined to replace the fine-nibbed pen) and drew characters that were supposed to come out bigger. It "had changed the spirit of the drawing."[12] The artist-writer began to enrich these "left-handed exercises" with ever-greater quantities and varieties of blotches, alterations, and violent markings so as to produce a sense of intense chaos. Now covering large sheets of paper, the marks gathered in magnificent "battles" that were waged at the margin between verbal and graphic expression. In fact, language as existential space was a battlefield that preoccupied him during his whole life. The work's intensity and poignancy is perceptively described by Maurice Blanchot:

> If Henri Michaux's inventions strike us as so close to us and speak so directly to our fate, even though they do not seem to implicate us at all, it is first of all because they symbolize this general condition of our destiny, namely, that it can only discover a meaning in its attempts to escape from this meaning and indeed from all possible meaning altogether—so that the sheer gratuitousness of his fictions and sometimes of his language is what matters to us the most. But, at the same time, this gratuitousness, this objectivity without resonance, this blind and dumb placidity are all part of a movement whose other extremity discloses the power of anger and of tempestuousness, anxiety and despair, infinite emotion. There is no other contemporary work where human anxiety and failure have found an expression at once more reserved and more violent, or a voice more proud and more tragic.[13]

When René Bertelé pointed out to Michaux that in *Mouvements* drawing and writing are not equivalent, the former being freer and the latter more dense, the artist responded:

> There's nothing astonishing about that. They are not the same age. The drawings are quite new in me, especially these, in the very process of being born, in the state of innocence, of surprise; but the words, the words came afterwards, afterwards, always afterwards ... and after so many others. How could they set me free? On the contrary, it is through having freed me from words, those tenacious partners, that the drawings are frisky and almost joyous, that their movements came buoyantly to me even in exasperation. And so I see in them a new language, spurning the verbal, and so I see them as *liberators*.[14]

Few are more conscious and eloquent than Michaux about the relationship between the written text and its liberating counterpart, drawing. Seemingly prefiguring the conceptual artist, he reflects publicly in essays and poetic aphorisms about his work and the world.

Therefore, a book dedicated to his work—in this case the exhibition catalogue from The Drawing Center—should begin with Michaux's position as a draftsman and a writer who worked with a wide spectrum, from the merely visible to the highly legible.

Insofar as Michaux considers drawing as a discourse of enactment and writing as a discourse of knowledge, his position can be compared to what Giorgio Agamben describes in Western culture as the fundamental scission of the word, the notion "that poetry possesses its object without knowing it while philosophy knows its object without possessing it. The word is thus divided between a word that is unaware, as if fallen from the sky, and enjoys the object of knowledge by representing it in beautiful form, and a word that has all seriousness and consciousness for itself but does not enjoy its object because it does not know how to represent it."[15] However, Michaux, who was fascinated by nonrational experiences and non-Western traditions, tried again and again to upset the old imperatives of differentiation between drawing and writing by developing a continuous exchange and acknowledging that both follow the same creative logic and desire in the inscriptive gesture of tracing. Above all, this process is about the hand exploring a given space, traveling over the paper, and organizing it according to its own possibilities. "The genesis of the text, as of any written mark (particularly that of drawing), must be considered from the viewpoint of the original spatial play which the hand stages. Neither the paradigm of the eye nor that of language allows us to grasp the meaning of 'first draft' dynamics—the moment when its enunciation is born in distinction from what it enunciates. The paradigm of the hand, however, achieves such an understanding. Originally what is at stake in the hand is the very nature of the psychic investments which are bound up in it."[16] In the tracing process Michaux often intended to blur the distinctions between writing and drawing by incorporating ideogrammatic signs, the alphabet, and calligraphic marks, while removing them from the duty of representation or connotation. He altered and played with the forms of language until they disappeared into continually changing fragments of movement, creating a new, visual language to communicate the disruptive and inchoate. Through fluid works, Michaux attempted to return the lines and strokes to a pre-symbolic, pre-linguistic state. There thus emerges a sort of truth of the hand, which requires drawing to show everything without dissimulation, without cheating, without trickery.[17] Paradoxically, this ethical dimension construes drawing as fidelity to the dictates of an idea and emphasizes its instrumental function as the signifier corresponding to the signified. This, of course, goes back to the Renaissance conception of drawing as *idea* and brings us further toward the recent claims of conceptual art, which has again attempted to radicalize drawing as the expression of an idea and its processes of coming-into-being. This characteristic would seem to rejoin writing and drawing, charging both of them with the expression of thought, of clarity, of black-on-white. Posited as a pure vehicle for content, however, this conception of drawing neglects the bodily impulses present in elementary traits or strokes. It is the perception of the double bind that makes Michaux's all-embracing œuvre even more fascinating. The bi-fold unraveling of the artist's gestural lines and distorted articulations produces a non-discourse that undercuts linguistic systems. "Moving further and further away from mimesis, represent-ation, and narration, Michaux's languages, seemingly stemming from the same body, finally merge or at least collapse. His audience is asked to perceive, read, decipher lines pertaining neither to a familiar alphabet nor to a recognizable outline and defying the principles of repetition and analysis."[18] Devoting his whole mind to the concept and his whole soul to the image, he tries to reconcile their contradictory impulses into an impossible synthesis: "the image cannot give matter to the concept; the concept, by giving stability to the image, would stifle its existence."[19]

The dialectics operative in Michaux's work seem to epitomize the literal passages in twentieth-century drawing from the more gestural expression of the unconscious to the conceptualization of a form of thought. In this sense, the exhibition *Untitled Passages by Henri Michaux*, which connects these polarities and includes work from the 1920s through the 1970s, has been conceived as an imaginary hinge between the first and second part of the twentieth century represented by two historical exhibitions at The Drawing Center: the first exhibition—*The Prinzhorn Collection: Traces upon the Wunderblock* (with drawings from the 1890s to the 1920s)—being about the line drawn *beyond* reason, and the forthcoming exhibition about drawing in minimalism and conceptualism (with work from the 1960s, 1970s, and 1980s)—being about the line drawn *within* reason. Through this series, The Drawing Center attempts to expose various developments in twentieth-century drawing. A challenging exploration rather than a conventional historical survey, the series considers drawing as it emerged in different contexts of space and time. Through research in lesser-known areas of visual production, each of the exhibitions reiterates a decisive moment of the development of drawing throughout the era of modernity. Although the exhibition sequence is dedicated to specific topics and moments, this way of working allows flexibility and open-endedness in the analysis of the subject of drawing—paralleling the medium of drawing itself—and as such it does not claim to establish one reading but to induce many readings.

Since the Michaux exhibition is not conceived of as a retrospective, it includes primarily non-figurative works that explore drawing as an outlet for expression beyond and within the limits of language. Rather than strictly following a chronology, the display traces the rhythms permeating the work with repetitions, pauses, jumps, disappearances, and resurgences—in the manner of a dance. The exhibition takes its name from Michaux's large body of *untitled* drawings (ones released from descriptive burden) and one of his books of poetic writings, *Passages*. In seeking to combine the two art forms, the exhibition investigates to what extent the boundaries between the fields of literature and art can be crossed, and proposes a timely reconsideration of Michaux's creative process. He worked to transcribe what some poets call the "inner phrase," a sort of palpitation that resists expression but that bears witness to the passage of life within a person as well as to the continuous passage from the real to the imaginary. The exhibition espouses this same kind of movement and emphasizes the connections in Michaux's work between the abandonment of the self within a floating world devoid of points of reference and the concern for the unfolding of visual and written expression on the blank page.

In 1998 The Drawing Center initiated its research into the line between the literary and the visual through the exhibition *Shadows of the Hand: The Drawings of Victor Hugo*. When one views work by artist-writers such as Victor Hugo and Henri Michaux, it becomes clear that the writing process, as it follows the line of thought to which it gives form, can be considered a practice forever on the point of drifting off course. "This appears during the pauses and hesitations of the thought process, when the pen can be caught accomplishing other gestures: additions, scribbles, and the excessive embellishment of letters, the transformation of words, lines, and inkblots into heads, animals, or other, less creditable things—'the hand talks' says Dubuffet. The visible returns and jostles with the legible: it is unpretentious, playful, useless, and it draws writing towards mocking."[20] This unconstrained relationship between writing and drawing may nonetheless be lost in the transformation from the handwritten manuscript to the digitized text. What the penstroke linked together, the keystroke seems to set apart. As the hand uses different inscriptive instruments, ranging from the pencil to the typewriter to the computer, its gestures follow the same itinerary during the thought process, but all its deviating traces are erased on the screen, drawn into invisibility. The legible becomes too legible. The whole conceptual process of marking is effaced and results in a perfect pristine soft or hard copy to be delivered without stains, without marginalia …

Still, at least potentially, the current technological revolution seems to bring the computer closer to the conditions of manual creation than the typewriter had done before, because the latter excluded the many operations to be performed quickly and easily by the hand, which the computer facilitates and stimulates. With the mouse one can indeed enter and exit the sentence at will in a myriad complex ways. Although within the normative use of standard word programs the array of diacritical marks is lost, there are far more possibilities for an active relationship with the computer that allows one to play and cut and paste and draw. At this moment such interfacing and engagement can also be recorded. Still, once the inscriptive gesture of tracing is mediated in this manner, one may wonder—and probably this question is triggered only by a certain nostalgia—what is going to happen down the road of digitalization and computerization to the fortuitous limbo between the legible and the visible—a limbo literally to be found in the margins on the pages of draft copybooks, at the direct intersection between writing and drawing. Often the traces ranged from simple graphic annotations and doodles to more elaborate sketches throughout the body of the manuscript, superimposed on the text or drawn on the back of the written pages. On the one hand this interspace between words and sketches dissolved the illusory barrier between the domain of literature and art, but on the other hand it constituted a sort of 'semiotic enclave' that could destroy literature as a finished product if it became visible. Over the course of centuries of technical improvements, typographical continuity, whereby the visual traces of the thought process have been concealed, has thus become more and more untouchable. Lost in virtual space, the trail of ink may no longer indicate the path taken by the traveler at the heart of darkness.

Acknowledgments

Many individuals have contributed to the realization of this exhibition, but there are two in particular to whom I owe a special acknowledgment. First and foremost, I thank the independent curator and art historian Florian Rodari, who co-organized this exhibition, a project that marks his return to The Drawing Center following his work on the Victor Hugo exhibition. Collaborating with Florian has been a profound pleasure and has included being the beneficiary of his great knowledge and love of poetry and language, a knowledge that he brings to bear on his inspired interpretation of visual art, particularly drawing. Florian has been the bedrock of this project, and I wish to express to him my heartfelt thanks. Equally important has been the tremendous generosity of Micheline Phankim. The success of this exhibition has been in large part due to her enthusiasm and goodwill. For her many gracious contributions to this project, I am deeply grateful.

This exhibition has been made possible through the remarkable generosity of our lenders, who have allowed critical artworks from their collections to become part of the fabric of the exhibition. In this respect, I wish to acknowledge the following private collectors: Pierre Alechinsky, Bougival, France; Claude Berri, Paris; Jean-Paul Croisier, Geneva; Mrs. Edwin Engelberts, Geneva; Mr. and Mrs. Claude Frontisi; Maurice Imbert, Paris; Catherine Putman, Paris; and Marie-Claude Tubiana, Paris, as well as those who have chosen to remain anonymous. In addition, I acknowledge the generosity of the following institutions and individuals, who agreed to join us as lenders to this project: Musée national d'art moderne, Centre Georges Pompidou, Paris, with deep thanks to Agnès de la Beaumelle, Curator, Department of Drawings; Musée de Valence, France, especially Hélène Moulin, Curator; Fonds régional d'art contemporain, Picardie, France, with particular appreciation extended to Yves Lecointre, Director; Fondation Maeght, with special thanks to Jean-Louis Prat; Mrs. Thessa Herold of the Galerie Thessa Herold, Paris; Cabinet des dessins des Musées d'art et d'histoire, Geneva, with thanks to Claire Stoullig, Curator; IVAM, Institut Valencià d'Art Modern, Spain, where we are indebted to Marta Arroyo, Coordinator; Musée de Grenoble, with thanks to Serge Lemoine, Chief Curator; and The Museum of Modern Art, New York, with gratitude and thanks to Margit Rowell, formerly the Chief Curator of the Department of Drawings.

The research undertaken by Florian Rodari and me necessitated that we prevail upon the expertise and assistance of a number of people. In particular, we should like to express our gratitude to those who have shared their insights on Michaux's art as well as to those who allowed us the privilege of viewing works first-hand. Here I wish to acknowledge: Alfred Pacquement, Director of the Centre Georges Pompidou and an expert on Henri Michaux's work; Catherine Lampert, Director of the Whitechapel Art Gallery, London; and Pierrette Turlais, at the Bibliothèque Nationale de France, Paris.

The spirited engagement of the entire staff at The Drawing Center has informed this undertaking at each step of its organization. Allison Plastridge, curatorial assistant and registrar, deserves special mention for sustaining us through this project by expertly handling—in French—innumerable details. For her immediate and ongoing contributions to this project I thank Elizabeth Finch, curator. With characteristic intelligence, Blair Winn, Development Associate, together with Rebecca Herman, Grant Associate, offered cogent strategic advice at key points along the way. Anne Blair Wrinkle, Development and Public Relations Associate, deserves our thanks for coordinating efforts to garner the public's interest in the project. The exhibition's installation has received the utmost attention from Linda Matalon, Director of Operations; Bruce Dow, an independent consultant; and Rachel Abrams, Operations Assistant. For their inspired development of education programs and public events, I thank Meryl Zwanger, Director of Schools Programs, and Lytle Shaw, Line Reading Series Curator, who also thoughtfully edited this text as it developed. In the past year and a half The Drawing Center's publications program has been greatly enlarged, and Katie Dyer, Assistant to the Director and Project Coordinator, has, with graceful alacrity, speed, and excellence, coordinated this publication, along with several other volumes and numerous *Drawing Papers*. For the design of this volume, I thank Luc Derycke and, for its publication and distribution, Hugh Merrell, Publisher; Matthew Hervey, Art Director; and Iain Ross, Editor at Merrell Publishers, London. It has been a pleasure to undertake another project with them. Cathy Carver, with the assistance of Malcolm Varon, completed most of the photography for this book, and we are indebted to their dedication to perfection.

We are most thankful for the exceptional degree of engagement demonstrated by the book's authors—Raymond Bellour (Professor, Ecole des Hautes Études en Sciences, Paris), Richard Sieburth (Professor of French and Comparative Literature, New York University), Florian Rodari, and Laurent Jenny (Professor, University of Geneva)—each of whom has provided a unique perspective on Michaux that has greatly enriched this endeavor. Leslie Jones has woven together an inspired and thorough chronology and an accompanying bibliography, which make significant contributions to this volume. For allowing us the opportunity to republish his interview with Michaux I thank the poet John Ashbery, who will also participate in a Line Reading event in conjunction with the exhibition. It is an honor to include his illuminating exchange with a poet and artist he so greatly admired. In addition to contributing to this book, Richard Sieburth has completed a beautiful translation of Michaux's *Émergences-Résurgences* that has been published in *Drawing Papers*, no. 13, in collaboration with Skira Publishers, Milan. Professor Sieburth undertook this monumental task with a vivid and nimble sense of language tuned faultlessly to the particularities of Michaux's poetic modes. Other translators who were commissioned by The Drawing Center for the essays in this publication are Alyson Waters and Christine Schmiedel, and I wish to thank them for their excellent and speedy work.

During the exhibition, The Drawing Center and the Maison Française, New York University, will be the hosts of a panel discussion on Michaux's work to be chaired by Denis Hollier, Professor of French Literature, New York University. Comprised of some of the catalogue's main authors (Professor Bellour, Professor Sieburth, Professor Jenny) and Professor Antoine Compagnon, this event offers an opportunity to gain new understanding of a celebrated figure who moved freely between the realms of poetry and the visual arts. For her interest in joining us as an organizer of this event I thank Francine Goldenhar, Director of the Maison Française of New York University.

In the last few years, The Drawing Center has been the beneficiary of the exemplary work of the French Cultural Services, which has encouraged the development of projects, such as our Victor Hugo exhibition, that bring renewed attention to exceptional individuals who have enriched French culture. At the French Cultural Services I am particularly grateful to Pierre Buhler, Cultural Counselor; Béatrice Ellis, Cultural Attachée; Antoine Vigne; Olivier Brossard; and Hervé Ferrage. The exhibition has been made possible by generous grants from them, along with the Eugene V. and Claire E. Thaw Charitable Trust, The Michel David-Weill Foundation, and agnès b. I am deeply appreciative of these funders for their early and sustained support. Finally, it has been both a pleasure and an honor to undertake this project with the unfailing guidance of The Drawing Center's Board of Directors. I extend special thanks to board members Edward H. Tuck and Elizabeth Rohatyn for their invaluable counsel and steady enthusiasm. Long champions of French arts and letters, they were quick to realize the value of this project devoted to a Belgian artist who came to make his home—and his many drawn and written marks—in France.

NOTES

1. Gaston Bachelard, *On Poetic Imagination and Reverie*, sel., trans., and intro. Colette Gaudin, Dallas, Texas (Spring Publications Inc.) 1987, p. 21.

2. Henri Michaux, *Passages*, trans. David Ball, Paris (Gallimard) 1963.

3. Henri Michaux, *Émergences-Résurgences* (1972), trans. Richard Sieburth, Milan (Skira) and New York (The Drawing Center) 2000, n.p.

4. Martine Reid, "Editor's Preface: Legible/Visible," *Boundaries: Writing and Drawing*, Yale French Studies, no. 84, 1994, p. 6.

5. Henri Michaux, "To Draw the Flow of Time," trans. Richard Fineberg, *Quadrum*, no. 3, Brussels 1957. Republished in *Henri Michaux*, exhib. cat., New York, The Solomon R. Guggenheim Museum, and Paris, Centre Georges Pompidou, Musée national d'art moderne, 1978, p. 98.

6. Henri Michaux, quoted in *Henri Michaux*, trans. John Ashbery, exhib. cat., London, Robert Fraser Gallery, 1963. First published in *Henri Michaux. Encres, gouaches, dessins*, exhib. cat., Paris, Galerie Daniel Cordier, October–November 1959.

7. *Ibid*.

8. David Ball, *Darkness Moves. An Henri Michaux Anthology: 1927-1984*, Berkeley and Los Angeles, California, and London (University of California Press) 1994, pp. xii–xiii.

9. Henri Michaux, *Par des traits*, Paris (Fata Morgana) 1984.

10. Ball 1994, pp. xii–xiii.

11. "Ce qu'a dit Francis Bacon à David Sylvester" in the journal *Derrière le miroir*, no. 162, November 1966, p. 21. According to Alfred Pacquement's 1993 monograph (n. 42, p. 61), it originally came from a 1962 BBC interview with David Sylvester.

12. "To Draw the Flow of Time," Guggenheim/Pompidou 1978, p. 98.

13. Maurice Blanchot, *Henri Michaux ou le refus de l'enfermement*, Tours (Farrago) 1999, pp. 61–62. Excerpt trans. Richard Sieburth.

14. Henri Michaux, Postface, *Mouvements*, ed. René Bertelé, Paris (Collection Le Point du Jour, Gallimard) 1951.

15. Giorgio Agamben, "Stanzas: Word and Phantasm in Western Culture," trans. Ronald L. Martinez, *Theory and History of Literature*, LXIX, Minneapolis and London (University of Minnesota Press) 1993, p. xvii.

16. Serge Tisseron, "All Writing is Drawing: The Spatial Development of the Manuscript," *Boundaries: Writing and Drawing*, Yale French Studies, no. 84, 1994, p. 29.

17. Georges Roque, "Writing/Drawing/Color," *Boundaries: Writing and Drawing*, Yale French Studies, no. 84, 1994, pp. 47–48.

18. Renée Riese Hubert, "Derrida, Dupin, Adami: 'Il faut etre plusieurs pour ecrire,'" *Boundaries: Writing and Drawing*, Yale French Studies, no. 84, 1994, p. 244.

19. Bachelard 1987, p. 6.

20. Reid 1994, p. 7.

L'HOMME DE PLUME

Florian Rodari

However far he may have ventured—in his journeys abroad as well as in the spiritual realm—Henri Michaux always remained an *homme de plume*, a pen-man. While this French expression may be somewhat ironic, the remark itself is no way meant disparagingly. On the contrary, the instrument that this poet held in his hand throughout his life, and used as much in his writings as in the sketching of his drawings, remains one of the most mobile and daring, and at the same time one of the most precise and sobering, this century has given us. But in Michaux, there is an essential connection to the motion that guides the hand, lets it dangle or carries it to the sentence, to the line; this jumps out right away at someone reading him for the first time, or discovering one of his pieces hanging on the wall. A specific distance that everywhere and at all times reveals a *writing*, that is, a flow and, at the same time, an encountering of resistance.

Two sides have forever coexisted within the act of writing. The first, outwardly the most active of the two (or at any rate, the one that produces the greatest part of what we call literature), is in reality governed by discourse, conforming to the dictates of thought, to impulses of the heart or leaps of memory. But there is another side, admittedly one less familiar and less obvious, and which, without knowing it, responds to the fundamental motions of being. In the West, virtually nothing is done to allow time for the development of this part; hidden, resistant to logical proof, it is nevertheless a translator of innermost depths. Calligraphy (more fittingly named *the art of writing*, as practiced in the East, particularly in China), on the other hand, distinguishes between these two sides, exploiting both or even cultivating the second at the expense of the first. The calligrapher, mindful of every particle of both himself and the world—in the motion of his wrist, his entire body invested in the approach, through the ductility of the ink, the suppleness of the brush, the resistance of the paper—experiences a stillness, an extraordinary fusion, unimaginable in our own rational and authoritarian practice of writing. There is no need to recall the extent to which this sensual aspect of transcribed speech was lost with the advent of typography. Indeed, since the invention of type, or even further back, since laws have been engraved, since Latin epigraphy and its maxims inscribed in marble, it has trapped the written word within the silence and discipline of margins. This fierce will to regiment words, to place them in formations, registers, columns, lines, and squares—a veritable *police* (in French this word also refers to typeface) serving the orderly mind and limited time—contrasts with the sand writing of the East and its astounding ability to condense into a single mark the expressiveness of gesture, and the distant echo of a sense.

From his very first texts, the poet Henri Michaux set out to eliminate the authoritarian complexity of institutionalized language in his writings, this pompous, morbid, rigid, and dreadfully pretentious side that contaminates men's speech the moment they use it to judge, affirm, or direct. Right from the outset and for the duration of his life, he longed to replace this *glu*, invoked in one of his first poems ("*et glo/ et glu/ et deglutit sa bru .../*"), with a mobility, a suppleness, a relativism more in keeping with life and its motion. From *Qui je fus*, published in 1927, onwards, Michaux devises a writing which is resolutely *against*.

True, words seemed to have fallen from grace when this young writer of the 1920s was choosing his mode of expression. Those who, like Michaux, were about to use them in a Europe still reeling from the rifts of war suspected words of having failed in their task, of henceforth disappointing and not being appropriate for describing the urgency and ruin opened up by the collective insanity. The effectiveness that had for so long been theirs— bringing men together by ensuring the continuity of a viable social order—was seriously shaken. The more demanding denounced the failure of this logical world, established in part by words and perpetuated by them for centuries. Despite the rare precision of the verbal tool very quickly in his possession, a precision immediately recognized by his elders, Michaux soon felt the need, as did so many of his peers in this era, to stake his precocious talent, to subject his means of expression to standards other than those of success or power. Thus, he soon wanted to divert his natural talent for description, as well as his delight in writing and playing with words, passed down from his first real emotions, his passions as a reader, to put them to work for a higher purpose, one dictated from within by the artist's ever-unquenched desire for truth.

The fact remains that words, uniquely, belong to a code that one may not jettison without fear of ending up in an aporia, in a sterile solipsism; it is for this reason, no doubt, that Michaux never followed the example of André Breton and his Surrealist friends in their automatic-writing experiments. His most extreme attempts, in scorn or anger, always retain a tie with the communication system in which he has agreed to express himself. His attacks against apathy and the established order, however frequent and scathing they may be, never call into question the foundations of language. Indeed, in his eyes, language is defined by a structure that requires sense, be it absurd, be it even *non*sense. Admittedly, the mediocrity of relationships, the weakness of feeling, and shortsightedness remain the meager lot that falls to those who choose to use words; but nothing can be done to escape from this self-enclosed system, in many ways a remarkable one, but nonetheless enclosed. Michaux was too much a writer entirely to forego their company, however imperfect or disabled they may be, and it was precisely in the often-made criticism of this disability that he would derive the best parts of his written work.

Fairly quickly, however, Michaux decided to entrust the task of probing those depths that words, too slow and ill-equipped, cannot reach, to the obscure, ignored part of the drawing hand. The effects of this decision, made in the state of shock that followed a revealing encounter with certain images, daydream-generated profitable displacements of Klee and Max Ernst, was meteoric; the catch, immediate and miraculous. Freed of its obligation to serve rational discourse, the spontaneous and unexpected rush carrying it along despite itself, the hand immediately experienced a joyous certainty, one often reiterated by Michaux. What is more, this suddenly acquired speed allowed it to discover domains that are utterly inspiring. The celebrated *dessins à fond noir* (the black backgrounds), drawings on black grounds that date from the late 1930s, are eloquent in this respect. Here we see the playing out of a writing before the alphabet, before the 'cretinizing' of the child through the acquisition of communication codes. Here the world is still without barriers, without language or gender distinction, stripped of its fatal inclinations. It is returned to its origin, into the space of its beginnings, a moving darkness in which strange primordial motions are stirred up and where ritual circles are formed of which we are no longer a part, but the importance of which seems to us nonetheless obvious. "Black is my crystal ball," Michaux once said, even before beginning to draw, and from this opaque darkness he foresees life being able to "come out." The black space contains images, just as the sheet of paper irresistibly attracts them. Right away, Michaux seems to assert, the drawing pen allows us to return to our most distant childhood, to recover in ourselves the very depths where irrational terror coexists with the simplest of joys.

There is no doubt that in Michaux's eyes, at least in the early years of his career, painting was to have the advantage of opening up an unknown continent, one unmarred by points of reference and uncluttered with ancestors. What is more, it offered horizons of fantastic, unhoped-for proportions, compared with corseted, booby-trapped, old-fogey literature; horizons where the hand, youthful and wide-open, must have found it possible to race off, fancy-free, in a resolutely beneficial state of ignorance.

Intimacy of size is the first thing that engages the eye of the individual who steps forward to the discovery of these works: pocket-sized paintings one must read up close, hand-held paintings more suitable for a portfolio consultation than the wall of a gallery. Right away, the notion of the page to be read and of the book emerge in the same proportion of familiarity and convenience: no studio, no huge canvasses. A minimum of equipment. Limited to oneself. On the flat of the desk. What is more, Michaux's preferred support is paper, its easily manipulated lightness making it for all things an ideal partner, used sometimes for its absorbent quality, sometimes for its high resistance and sheen. Obviously, the posture of one who approaches a sheet of paper lying flat before him is not the same as that of the painter attacking a canvas from an upright position and thus in an altogether different relationship of confrontation. Here, having no model, the artist has only to bend over himself.

For a long time, fine-tipped pens and paintbrushes, Indian ink, washes, watercolor, and gouache, which require no major equipment, were Michaux's only instruments. Chosen for the ease with which they can be handled, as well as for their ability to respond to internal pressure, they allow the hand to react quickly and subtly to the impulse of the wrist, to carry out the gesture, confined to sense and space, that can be qualified as writing. In calligraphy —this is in fact one of its rudiments—gestures do not have to be sweeping ones, they need only mobilize maximum, but contained, power, as well as maximum sensibility. The ink can flow through the air or drift, it all depends, but in any case it seems to be without fetters. Oil painting, more deliberate, clings to the ground, does not break free. And when, rather belatedly, it was used by Michaux, it was in fluid flat tints, or in short, nervous accents; never in thick, slow-drying pastes.

At regular intervals throughout his work as a painter, Michaux devoted himself to pages of writing, where signs, motions, ideograms, whatever we want to call them, show a considerable ease, a freedom of gesture seemingly boundless. There is never any repetition: an absolute steadiness in this hand running wild ensures the autonomy of each of these forms, which, while related, share no family resemblance, sign-cells in which the muscular energy varies according to time and ink. An instinctive knowledge of the body as well as a blind faith in space are constantly visible in these pages; an extreme build-up that promotes the uncontrollable outburst of the hand, which dances and races across the sheet, covering its area. In this space as well, the pen aids flight.

In contrast to these small and deliberate black grenades that grab the eye, the colors used by Michaux are, in general, seldom conclusively asserted. Prissy pinks, brownish and olive-greenish tints, celadons, pale turquoises, saffron yellows, glints rather than sources of light, and in truth not very straightforward, rather cowardly, almost sickly—these all do their part to send the gaze into a state of indecision, a perceptible wavering between well-being and uneasiness, always irresponsible. Applied as translucent glazes, these colors never clearly coincide with a form: they are tints rarely seen in the Western world, barely even tints for that matter, in any case defying any commonly held definition one might have of them. And this slight skewing of our habitual modes of perception reinforces all the more the sense of improbability conveyed by these colors. The only semblance of order is provided by a sort of interplay of three voices, tone responding to tone, in the monotony of colors: a harmonic repetition that revitalizes the disintegration and gives a vague sense to the mess.

In these works, then, one is first struck by the modesty of means, the lack of materials, the sobriety of effects. They seem to be made of nothing, sometimes even less. The speed surprises as well, curiously recalling not so much haste as extreme distance. One comes across forms that are reluctant to be fixed, charged with a dynamism that for all of its intensity does not provide any direction. The meanings cling to glass without asserting themselves, or with a slowness that fails to persuade. One makes out, as mentioned, colors that are just barely colors, little glazes of drab wash grazing the surface of the paper or fabric, giving the impression of delicacy, of precariousness, of hesitancy to commit. Everywhere, we see volition abdicating and entrusting the initiative to the support, to the ink; if necessary, to accidents like folds, smudges, blots, mishaps. The artist seems satisfied just to witness their mutual metamorphoses, exploiting the disturbance of the projected drawing caused by the encounters of pigment and liquid in watercolors as well as the thirst of the paper. The work must develop on its own, before the eyes of the one hatching it, who pays it extreme attention but intervenes only at a minimum. Even the page itself never holds firmly to its margins: it, too, floats, punctuated by drawings that show little respect for the approximate order they attempt to impose. Thus, in these works, order is constantly fighting the refusal to accept order; logic opposes the refusal to accept logic. Thus, familiarity alternates with strangeness; the two sometimes overlap, to the point where one ends up feeling as if the systematic disturbance of space that strikes these images is nothing more than respect for an order imposed from further away—a higher order, but one that is always escaping the body, escaping the mind, one that is always on the run, unfathomable, elusive. But if one loses oneself in it for a few minutes, all sorts of very ancient, vital sensations resurface, and the treasures usually eclipsed by sight reassert themselves: materials, sounds, even smells that seem to re-emerge from this contemplation—muffled, but forcefully beating out their forgotten rhythm.

Admittedly, his books also touch upon this turbulent infinity (*L'Infini turbulent*), this world of absence, this "elusive world, well-known, immense and immensely perforated, in which everything is, and at the same time is not, in which everything shows and does not show, contains and does not contain" (*Émergences-Résurgences* [Éditions d'art Albert Skira] 1972, p. 106); more precisely, a world in which everything collapses the more one moves forward, and where paradox prevails. One can recognize some of the same qualities in Michaux's language, as well as a similarly unsettling power, obtained by the most modest of means. Thus, when he describes awkward situations in his texts—like those in which his heroes are trapped despite themselves and, in a way, because of the very fact of their being— or coolly cruel actions by which he seeks to disorient the reader and propel him beyond his natural borders, it is with his writing pen, and through very much the same minute deviations obtained by his paintbrush, the same slight unlikelihoods, those mistakes just slightly off the mark, those slippages of logic, which are not too far from the sad realities of life. Certain descriptions, for example those depicting the *Meidosems*, or even the accounts of Plume's sorry adventures, possess the irritating characteristic of immediately tumbling into the absurd, of invariably inviting disappointment, of having no outline, of dissolving into the worthless, the empty, the useless. And for good measure, they have the ability to reveal the darkest, most hideous secrets of being, its most ridiculous aspects, its pointless bustling about, its petty outcome, its fears and cowardices.

Nevertheless, as Michaux has many times repeated, by trading his writing pen for the drawing brush he was seeking to escape from the sense that magnetizes words, fixing them inexorably to their destiny within the sentence and determining their forward movement. All of a sudden, he was demanding space, but space without aim—without delay, without restrictions. And yet, surely the poetry he had been working on for years, the poetry of *Qui je fus*, of *La Nuit remue*, of *Voyages en Grande Garabagne*, provided ample amounts of this space? Yes, but not on the same terms. For painting—a territory that was still largely unfamiliar to him, or at any rate, relatively uncharted in his eyes—above all else allowed him the freedom of an exercise in which each new event, each formal or semantic accident spontaneously appearing on the paper or canvas became an unexpected pleasure, delight, stimulation, the creation of a field of possibilities that writing seemed henceforth incapable of achieving at this speed or with such joy. In painting, there is no longer any prerequisite for description, and description no longer owes anything to a language system: very naturally it discovers itself through gesture and the unpredictability such gesture bears within itself.

Whatever the poet might have done with phrases and lines in his attempt to convey the drift he felt (in himself or in things), or better still to stimulate the loss of all ties that he wished to achieve, at some point words inevitably caught up with him, re-fastened him to some edge, kept him from falling. He should have kept quiet—this Michaux knew perfectly well. For to speak is to refuse to let oneself drift off entirely; it is to keep a link with sense, with the earth, with others, the familiar, the norm, despite whatever efforts might be made to destroy these authorities within oneself. Notwithstanding this, was Michaux ever for a moment tempted to be silent? Never. The transition into painting, on the other hand, allowed him to restore a balance that had been upset, to meet an expectation. It was also the result of an extraordinary openness and thirst for knowledge, two elements that, together, would later lead him to embark on other courses and, specifically, to experiment with mescaline.

Pen still in hand, seated in the same place, blackening the same paper, never really changing his gesture, nor his distance above the sheet, Michaux slid very quickly, more quickly even than was for a long time imagined, into the adventure without words, the adventure without restraint that is drawing. And even if elements of the familiar world came back to him along the way—men's faces, landscapes, animals—even if analogies with his poems are constantly apparent, it was in spite of him: it was because the body's memory had henceforth gotten hold of these elements and was giving them back, above and beyond any conscious will. From the moment Michaux devoted himself to painting, as he saw it, all he had to do was follow; at this stage, he was no longer directing anything; it was no longer even him loading the pen with ink. Instead, he was carried by the fluid, agreeing to let himself be swept away, literally taken for a ride.

As soon as he grabs hold of his paintbrush, all filters disappear—this is something he has said, written, and repeated. Having pushed out of the way, once and for all, the delays caused by verbal explanations, the concessions made to syntax, and all the clever metaphors, the painter was now able to free an image that was closer to the truth he hoped to reach. Not a more knowing image, but one that is more vibrant, more carnal, a heart heavier with blood, with sap. Watercolor and Indian ink alike, both selected for their ductility, seem to quiver at being thus displayed in the raw. Henceforth, any irony is involuntary, though it may seriously wound; as if painting tore down all the defenses and rendered anguish and the tragic element more vulnerable, as well as more imminent. Here, terror is no longer just an image. Things are no longer a laughing matter. One has traveled into the inside of pain, of the scream, of the throat. Outbursts and panic seem to lie at the tip of the paintbrush, which through capillary attraction worms its way into the most intimate interstices of the wound, going back to the source of primordial violence. The world, in its trembling, in its erotic splendor, surfaces; it imposes its horrible and fascinating redness.

In these images, one also comes across the tattered populations of Michaux's poems, those beings that tear each other to pieces, gesticulating in the void, brandishing their pipe dreams against forces as futile and dazed as themselves. But from this point on, their struggle has something tragically definitive about it, and all the more so since everything that appears before the gaze is singularly lacking in the capacity to make itself register. These figures look quite like men, or rather some kind of human form with a head, arms, and hands, but this is never a very convincing resemblance. They are more similar to the homunculus, the runt, the rag doll; and when gathered in a crowd—which might give them an illusion of reality—they never really show solidarity, never advance in the same direction: they don't even look alike; every figure is out for itself. Finally, when faces appear, they are disfigured, bruised masks. Nor does the drawing ever assert itself in structures or in solids. Its forms sometimes recall the fragile plant shucked and scattered in the wind: filaments, frayed clouds. At other times they remind us of the amniotic kingdom where microscopic animals, protozoa, spermatozoa, hard to distinguish in the cloudy liquid, propel themselves with a sudden flip of the tail behind a rock, or bury themselves in the sand. Every apparition suggests a pre-uterine, abyssal life, an aquarium life that is therefore rarefied, wasted, not yet settled in its being nor in its place. Even more rarely do the figures have a center; what one takes for their eyes might just as well be a naval or a genital. There is no link to the ground, no sediment, no organization. Even repetition, one of Michaux's leitmotifs, never guarantees the presence of a causality. Faces, the sole reference points in the uncertainty of watercolors, sometimes emerge from the quick knots that the painter elicits from the primordial soup, and that he stretches into dribbling blots, his pen nonchalantly reconstructing a coherence, though only a minimally acceptable one. The faces emerge unexpectedly along the way, under the path of the brush. And still the pupil has some difficulty adjusting its perception to their form, in the same way that one must progressively adjust to seeing poorly in the dark, or to distinguishing things when dazzled by the sun. Their blurred outlines bring about spatial hallucinations and category confusions. One is haunted by them, never knowing when they will emit their faint signal, or what forms they will take. All one knows is this: indecisive, these faces evolve as accidental events, dictated by the motions of the brush and the properties of the materials. Guided by some secret instinct, the eyes, the nose, and the mouth position themselves in the right places, but that is as far as this goes. Determinateness and resemblance stop there, and it is precisely this that brings about the strong uneasiness and distressing expressive force of these images, not to mention their heaviest load of anxiety. For what could be more distressing than a face that looks like you, could even be your own, but at the same time remains radically foreign, the inverse of a double, with a fixed stare, a wild look, scrutinizing a place elsewhere, beyond or below our habitual horizon; worse yet, scrutinizing aimlessly, more precisely, with no intention at all.

At this stage of contemplation, all resistance is useless. We must in our turn agree to this frightened descent into a space without points of reference, tourists in realities still foreign to us, and guided in this drift by psychopomp figures reduced to a measly glimmer, a tremendously vague and tremendously passive round mass, remote, ageless, voiceless, merging with the origin to which we will never have access, not even by surrendering everything to it. Here, we are no longer provided with the criteria that allowed us to catch our breath, to resist, while reading texts. Here, the vibrational motion of forms and the disappearance of spatial axes are far too divorced from any known code for us to be able to keep ourselves from falling headlong, totally at a loss.

Beware of the poet! Such is the warning that was often pronounced in reference to the paintings and drawings of Henri Michaux. It is a warning that he himself heard on more than one occasion and that, understandably enough, irritated him. As if it were not appropriate for an artist, already active and almost confirmed in one art, to venture into another; as if each of us were dealt only one hand in the game ... Michaux, inveterate explorer of himself and the world, worked relentlessly to destroy this absurd prejudice by working at the same time as a painter and a writer. His entire body of work demonstrates that the two facets of the hand-with-pen may not be dissociated from one another; that often they are interwoven, more frequently even than one has sometimes been willing to admit; finally, that their double presence is necessary if one is to dispense once and for all with this pointless separating of different genres within a single man, within one and the same desire. But which of these facets will have the upper hand in this conquest is never entirely predictable. Thus, on the occasion of his voyage into mescaline country some years later, the two courses offered by the art of writing were successively taken in order to recount the effects of drugs on the gaze. And if at first sight the hand—drawing, subjected to impulse—appears to be the ideal seismograph, capable of recording with virtual simultaneity the slightest jolts in the body's temporarily altered functions, no one could predict that the distanced discourse of *a posteriori* evaluation would provide such a precise and rich report on the experience. The accounts found in numerous drug-related texts such

183

as *Misérable miracle, Connaissance par les gouffres*, and *Face aux verrous*, in endeavoring to find a verbal equivalent of the vision experienced, are often more eloquent than the drawings, which can seem rather repetitive. The lucidity, mediacy, and mastery of writing thus provide a tremendous pendant to the approach by drawing, somehow inadequate, strangely faint compared with the dazzling experience related in the textual accounts, and somewhat frozen, as if overcome by the unique effort of retracing the tremors, the simultaneously minuscule and obsessive movements occupying the pupil of the alkaloid-altered subject. The inexhaustible richness of visions, the inexhaustible combinations of motion, the expansions of spatial reality—all of these are conveyed by the texts:

> By flashes of zigzags, by flashes of transversal flights, by flashes of lightning streaks, I see things pronounced, go into hiding, assert themselves, assure themselves, forget themselves, get a hold back on themselves, steady themselves, by flashes of punctuation, of repetition, of hesitant jolts, by slow deviations, by fissurings, by imperceptible slippages, I see it forming, deforming, re-deforming itself, an edifice in the making, in perpetual metamorphosis, and transubstantiation, now assuming the form of a gigantic larva, now appearing the first project of an immense and almost orogenic tapir, or the still quivering loincloth of a black dancer who has collapsed and is about to fall asleep. But surging from sleep, and even before sleep sets in, the magnificent edifice re-emerges in all of its magnificence, its articulations recast in rubber.
> [*Misérable miracle*, Paris (Collection Le Point du Jour, Gallimard) 1972, p. 41]

Speed and motion: exclusive privilege of the draughtsman? The syntax and prosody of the poet in these admirable passages are no doubt just as capable of describing the sumptuous chaos invading the mescaline-influenced mind as are the artist's wrist and ink-filled brush, in their attempt to follow the trembling of the visible and to conjure it up in the form of plausible signs. One recognizes here the tireless curiosity exuded by an artist, widening space as he goes along cutting a path for himself, opening and reshutting doors, coming, going, returning to his starting point, setting off again. One admires the fact that it is not only under the paintbrush that wonders and demons appear, and that the theatre of within is not the exclusive prerogative of painting. Indeed, if painting was able, when the time came, to reconjure up all sorts of buried strata that would be unimaginable in the broad daylight of writing, certain sentences, certain inflexions in the rhythm, certain turns of phrases, sweeping the reader along in their motion, bullying him with all sorts of violent and unusual metaphors, arousing fear or anguish in the course of a description, are equally disturbing, equally revealing. In Michaux, the distinction made between the two active parts of the hand was bound to end in this fusion, so close do the relations between them remain, so shared their inquiries. *Émergences-Résurgences*, a book of written remarks that relate Michaux's experience as a painter, left in the care of editor Albert Skira for his collection *Les Sentiers de la création*, provides the most convincing illustration of the fusion. Here, the two approaches conform ideally to one another, without ever letting go of their respective individuality, explaining each other, mingling their rhythms and their treasures.

In order to achieve self-knowledge and to widen our perspective on the world, in order to explore the incomprehensible diversity of the workings of humans, no way is insignificant nor invariably preferable to another. Given the time, Henri Michaux would have further increased the number of his paths of approach—whether or not these paths would have been tolerated, dreadful, or even dangerous is really of no importance. What does matter for this body of work, and for us, the reader/viewers, is that the drawings, the watercolors, the gouaches, or the oil paintings; the poems, the narratives, and the analyses all lead near to what we are in our secret depths, near to the breath of inspiration from which we start to live again, near to the innermost source from which we begin to speak, to see. Like many of his contemporaries, Michaux was persuaded that an operation needed to be performed on habits and ordinary passions; a sort of excision or revitalization of every perceptible channel that gives access to the worlds that mold us. But in his estimation, the artist should set the example, that is, start with himself. Constant self-mutilation, constant descent. Tumbling to the bottom, turning off all of the lights. Silencing the noises to which his very art had given life, with the exception of those that form a sort of vague vegetative and impersonal continuum; ending all manifestation of his self, *conditio sine qua non* of an actual approach. And in this naked state, without any reference points, before and beyond all identity, wholly abandoned, but without regrets, despite oneself, allowing new paths, new directions to take shape; paths and directions which the pen—but just as well as any other instrument— redraws, letting words or signs escape. At this stage of non-participation, having provoked a state of emptiness (by deliberate intoxications, meditation, contemplation, suffering, despair), an extraordinary movement arises, and a life unbelievably rife with jolts, withdrawals, doublings, and expansions once again becomes possible. Suddenly a link is re-established, on the condition, once more, of renouncing the possession of all things, or the exercise of all powers, of agreeing to participate in (without really being in a position to, nor wanting to modify its flow) the slow, imperceptible trepidations within. To be the active witness of all the desires that have collapsed, of all the blurred forms that will never exteriorize themselves, of all the faces which will remain in the larval state, of all the motions that will never take place in space, of all the times that will never happen in time. It was only by agreeing to play the left-hand part of his being, the uneducated, insolent part; it was only by relentlessly and fearlessly offering himself to the winds of the unknown, that Michaux managed to avoid the traps set by time, to rebel against the terrible prison of the real that forever holds things up, nails them down, and numbs. And this is the way his poems and drawings manage to convince and revive the most precious and solemn part of what lies within us, by continually jeopard- izing their own convictions. In their strange familiarity we recognize our own illusions, as much as our own weaknesses. They invite us on a tour of our mediocre conditions and our narrow territories. They are constantly ditching us, robbing us, but knowing just as well how to re-strengthen our desire to go and find out.

This victory was reaped by Michaux because he knew how to do battle on a terrain that is forever to be conquered, forever to be re-occupied, a terrain where man—free, active, and attentive, inner and outer—finally becomes able to hear, see, and love in the nakedness of the First Day, with the tenderness of one discovering the world as it was in the beginning, at once violent and splendid, before the division of the sexes. And if Michaux is still so close to us to this day, it is as much for this freedom as it is because he unceremoniously forces us to face ourselves, and this confrontation, cruel and embarrassing as it might be, beneficially causes us to re-examine all our assumptions. This kind of authority is only won through utter faithfulness to one's art—constantly pushing it to its limits, every day issuing new challenges that will later appear as so many conquests.

Henri Michaux in front of the studio-converted garage (Meudon), photographed by Maurice Fourcade, 1950

SIMPLE GESTURES

Laurent Jenny

Mɪᴄʜᴀᴜx ʙᴇɢᴀɴ ᴘᴜʙʟɪsʜɪɴɢ ɪɴ 1922. He started painting in 1925, probably after seeing a Surrealist exhibition where he had been able to discover the work of Paul Klee, Max Ernst, and Giorgio de Chirico. But it was not until 1936 that painting became a constant activity for him. There exists an Indian-ink fish, drawn in an almost calligraphic style, from 1925 and a large blot called *An Octopus or a City* (it does, in fact, resemble both an octopus and a map of Paris) from 1926, autographed for Jean Paulhan. Two drawings from 1927—the year his first collection of texts (*Qui je fus*; Who I Was) was published—are even more important, however, for establishing the origins of Michaux's pictorial project. In title and form, these drawings—*Alphabet* and *Narration*—clearly show the direction Michaux's aesthetic quest would take: his aim was to reconcile writing and drawing, which after all are both attributes of the same line, a line that is always liable to become shape or sign, to show or relate, or even to hesitate leisurely between the two. It was from this point on that Michaux, parallel to his literary work, would be preoccupied with developing a language of graphic signs, a kind of visual Esperanto. Fifty years after *Alphabet*, we still find this same preoccupation in a small booklet entitled *Idéogrammes en Chine*,[1] and again, just prior to his death, in the collection *Par des traits*,[2] where pages of drawings end with a meditation on the possibility of a graphic language. From the outset this language could be shared without having to be learned. It is "not really a language," writes Michaux, "but completely alive, more like emotions in signs that only distress and humor can decipher."

Although he never studied painting formally and rarely frequented artistic milieus, it would be naïve to think of Michaux as an 'outsider artist,' to believe that he somehow appeared, meteor-like, out of nowhere. Between 1925 and 1927 the essential aspects of Michaux's pictorial problematic were forged through contact with a few great works. There is no doubt, for example, that in those years he was absorbing the post-Symbolist theories of art that were in the air—those of Wassily Kandinsky, for example, for whom form "is a spiritual being endowed with the properties that are identified with it,"[3] and responds to an "internal necessity." Obviously, it is a long way from Kandinsky's spiritualism to Michaux's universe of psychic movements and apparitions. As we shall see, their "internal necessity" is not of the same order; but both Kandinsky and Paul Klee, Bauhaus theorists, could not fail to elicit Michaux's interest, working as they did to reveal the laws of a dynamic pictorial language. For them, forms are not inert traces but energetic movements that have their origins in internal tensions and are themselves producers of spatial tensions. And—this is the most 'modernist' aspect of their theory—the most basic elements of forms can, if necessary, be isolated in order to create an energetic alphabet. First formulated by the Bauhaus, this idea was in full bloom by the time Michaux began to work. As someone who created alphabets and sought out movement, Michaux could not have remained indifferent to it. In *Punkt und Linie zu Flache* (Point and Line to Plane),[4] Kandinsky devised a graphic language, creating it whole from a basic element shared by writing and drawing: the point, or period [*le point*]. An ambiguous element, both graphic minimum and diacritical mark, "the union of silence and speech," the period/point changes its logical value according to whether it is linguistic ("symbol of interruption, of non-being") or graphic ("the most concise and permanent affirmation, produced briefly, firmly, and quickly"). We find in Michaux's work a meditation on the logical values of affirmation and negation that are implied by form, but never an *a priori* theorizing. All of Michaux's plastic knowledge stems from *experience*, a word he uses to mean both experimentation—in which forms and materials are manipulated—and lived experience; that is, from an active reception of the unexpected nature of form.

Michaux's early painting is contemporary with yet another movement that may be qualified as post-Symbolist: Surrealism. Surrealism possessed both a means of expression, "pure psychic automatism," and an exploratory project: to render the "real functioning of thought." In the early days of Surrealism, the nature of this "thought" was still ill-defined: was it associative thought that had its origins in primary Freudian processes, or collective unconscious, or spiritualist message? As early as 1925 Michaux was already critical of Surrealism. In an article in the journal *Le Disque vert*,[5] he wrote ironically about the "incontinence" of Surrealism, its "unemotional" character, and its monotony. In his eyes, Surrealist automatism, "as monotonous as a clown," remained abstract and disincarnate. Its mechanical impersonality lacked body, just as it lacked a diverse, mobile subject. Further, and perhaps most importantly, painting had no place in the 1924 Surrealist Manifesto. At that time the very idea of a possible Surrealist painting was the subject of keen discussion among Surrealists in the pages of their journal, *La Revolution surréaliste*. There was heated debate between Pierre Naville and André Breton on the subject, but it was Max Morise who first clearly articulated the terms of this debate in an article of December 1924 entitled "Les Yeux enchantés."[6] The question was whether painting—the art of space—necessarily synthetic, calculated, and conscious of its own traces, was compatible with the spontaneous immediacy of psychic automatism. Practically speaking, there were three kinds of responses to this question, responses that were more or less legitimized by Breton in the articles he devoted to *Surrealism and Painting*, beginning in 1925:

abstract automatism, of which André Masson was virtually the sole representative;

Surrealist collage, as practiced by Max Ernst; and

oniric academicism, as illustrated at the time by de Chirico (and later, by Tanguy, Magritte, and Dalí).

There is no doubt that Masson's abstract automatism was the closest of all three to Michaux's preoccupations, although, as far as I know, Michaux never made reference to it. Masson drew in a trance-like state, stimulated by the intonation of support-words (such as "transmutation," "fall," and "whirlwind"). Later Masson would write:

The first graphic apparitions on paper are pure gesture, rhythm, incantation, and as a result: pure scribbling. That's the first phase./ In the second phase, the image (which had been latent), reclaims its rights. When the image has appeared, it is time to stop. This image is merely vestige, trace, wreckage.[7]

At least one of Michaux's drawings exists, reproduced in 1927 in the journal *Les Feuilles libres*, the tracing of which vividly calls to mind Masson's automatic drawings as they appeared in *La Revolution surréaliste*[8] at the time. Michaux was surely not indifferent to the spontaneity of

Masson's gestures. But he had also keenly observed the work of another Surrealist: Max Ernst. It was not Ernst the 'assembler'—the one who had totally reinvigorated the meaning of Cubist collage—who interested Michaux, but rather Ernst the 'visionary.'

Indeed, in August 1925 Ernst (re)discovered *frottage*: as he was contemplating the designs on a hotel-room floor, Ernst became obsessed with an idea from which he freed himself by rubbing a lead pencil across a piece of paper he had placed directly on the wooden floor. The images revealed were of forests, pampas, hordes of animals, and he collected them in his *Histoire naturelle* (1926). Later, he wrote that the artist here was a kind of "spectator, indifferent or passionate, at the origin of his work, who observes the phases of its development."[9] The idea of the revelation of a latent image was fundamental for Ernst, just as it had been for Masson. It would continue to haunt Michaux, who, much later, would take his inspiration from techniques promoted by Ernst, such as *frottage* and painting on a black background.[10] But the status of these latent images, and their relation to the subject, would preoccupy Michaux for a long time to come. If, then, Michaux did not really learn to paint, he *did* learn to look, and he is part of an 'expressive' pictorial trend that cuts across modernism and Surrealism: a quest for a pictorial language and a visual revelation of the unconscious.

Still, this trend would never have reached Michaux had not his personal history led him, by 'endogenesis,' to the necessity of certain gestures and sequences of gestures. This history must be retraced, or rather we must content ourselves with following Michaux, since he created his own originary myth. In 1929 a text entitled "The Son of the Macrocephalic" appeared in the journal *Commerce*. It was reprinted in 1930 in *Un certain Plume*, under the title "Portrait of A.," and, finally, in 1938 in *Plume*, in the section entitled "Difficulties." The autobiographical nature of this text is not in doubt since it can be verified by comparing it to other texts, in particular to a short text that Michaux wrote in 1959 for Robert Bréchon entitled "Some Information about Fifty-Nine Years of Existence."[11] A. is described in a bizarre psychological state, which must not be reduced summarily to contemporary psychiatric nosography:

> Up to the threshold of adolescence, he kept forming a hermetic and self-sufficient ball, a dense and personal and dim universe where nothing came in, neither parents, nor affections, nor any object, nor their image, nor their existence, unless they used force against him.[12]

But the relentlessness with which the doctors forced him to eat finally got through to A., bringing him to the end of what he believed to be a state of perfection, of sainthood almost.

> His perfect ball was anastomosed and even disintegrated visibly.
> A great languor, this ball. A great languor, a great slowness, a powerful rotation. An inertia, a mastery, an assurance. That particularly stable something that one encounters quite often in vices, or in morbid states.
> So the ball lost its perfection.
> Perfection gone, nutrition came, comprehension came. When he was seven years old, he learned the alphabet and ate.[13]

Still, the state of being a ball did not disappear but instead became externalized, deified, by means of a displacement:

> His first thoughts were of the person of God.
> God is ball. God is. He is natural. He must be. Perfection is. It is He. He alone is conceivable. He is. Furthermore, he is immense.[14]

Nutrition and the alphabet are thus interpreted as a fall, in the theological sense of the word; the 'ball' continues to exist, but at a distance from A. A. has not really been born, has not really entered the world. But born or not, he seeks a path to birth:

> He would like to act. But the ball wants perfection, the circle, repose. And yet he moves continually. From his ball a muscle emerges. He is happy. He will be able to walk, but a muscle by itself cannot create walking. Soon he becomes tired. He doesn't move any more. It is the evening of each day. In this way he has thousands of inceptions of muscles [*départs de muscles*]. It is not walking. He believes these inceptions will lead to walking. He is only a ball. He persists. He is on the lookout for movement. He is the fetus in a womb. The fetus will never walk. He must be made to come out, and that is something else entirely. But he persists, for he is a living being.[15]

This perfect, prenatal state continued to haunt Michaux under different guises—sleepiness, fatigue, laziness—and forced him to react in order to free himself from it. A text from 1950, entitled "Arriver à se reveiller," describes an effort that is repeated each morning, in which we find many aspects of A.'s difficulties. The self experiences itself as a corpse to be reanimated, or as a cloud, or a gaseous planet. It exhorts itself to find a form:

> Take heart! In this mass resides a will. This stubborn one without a body thrusts confusedly.[16]

If I have quoted so extensively from these texts it is because I believe they perfectly describe the universe of obstacles and impulses that governs Michaux's pictorial gesture. Viewed thus, painting was for Michaux a way of managing to wake up (or, if one prefers, a way of escaping sainthood). This act [*agir*], which is neither walking nor locomotion, this immobile act, this act to be born, creates what can be termed, as Michaux termed it, "inceptions of muscles" (one can hardly speak of 'drives,' unless it is in the most literal and almost pre-Freudian sense), and it will be realized in the imaginary life of the waking dream,[17] but also, increasingly, in painting, which in part realizes it materially.

Painting preserves both the integrity of the ball-state and the impulse to act. In the afterword to his collection *Mouvements* (1950–51), Michaux defines his work as a "reward of indolence." By means of a strange cleavage, the moving forms cause the body to experience extreme animation, all the while preserving, from below, its inertia:

> Their movement became my movement. The more there were of them, the more I existed. The more of them I wanted. Creating them, I became quite other. I invaded my body (my centers of action and repose). It's often a bit remote from my head, my body. I held it now, tingling, electric. Like a rider on a galloping horse that together make but one …
>
> Although this—must I say experiment? may be repeated by many, I should like to warn anyone who prizes personal explanations that I see here the reward of indolence.
>
> The greater part of my life, stretched out on my bed for interminable hours of which I never tired, I imparted motion to one or two or three forms, but always one more quickly, more to the fore, more diabolically quickly than any other. Instead of exalting it, investing it with riches, happiness, earthly goods as they are called, I gave it, as very poor as it remained in other respects, I instilled in it a quite extraordinary mobility of which I was the counterpart and the motor, albeit unmoving and slothful. Electrified it, while I myself was the despair of active people or the object of their scorn.[18]

Painting for Michaux may thus be defined as birth in labor. It will replay the self's negotiation with dissolution or compactness, inertia or movement, through the meeting of materials: the dissolving liquidity of watercolors, the rapidity of ink, the glue of gouache, and so on. Painting will decline in gestures every form of the act [*l'agir*]. It will also confront the subject with the formal and imaginary feedback that paper offers to it.

By taking into account this psycho-mythical background, we can sketch out an elementary poetics of Michaux's pictorial work. That is, we can distinguish in it a series of gestures that are never simply dynamic discharges, but also always movements of thought, logical positions of acceptance and refusal, of affirmation and negation. Michaux understood and identified this logical value of his gestures with a great deal of lucidity in the experience he had of forms. In this regard, he is at polar opposites to the theoretical approach of a Kandinsky or a Klee. There is no prior abstract theorizing for Michaux, but rather an attentive and suffering progression in gestures and forms. Here, each discovery is "vital," opening the way for or blocking the path of the one who is having trouble being born.

I identify in Michaux's work three kinds of gestures that imply values of affirmation or negation:

Tracing

Repelling

Revealing

It goes without saying that I am not trying to establish a chronological trajectory here: this succinct classification intends rather to show a logical development of his painting. In fact, Michaux did not especially paint by beginning at the beginning (or, rather, from 1927 on, he sketched out all beginnings at the same time); and I would add here that when one paints or writes the beginning can always be taken up again.

Tracing

The trace of the line in Michaux's work does not 'draw.' It translates the primary impulse to act. "In action I come [*Agir je viens*]," Michaux writes in one of his poems:[19] taking action and the impulse to take action are one and the same thing, since one comes to this act-taking and this act-taking is nothing other than a 'coming to,' in an intransitive dynamic. Here the verb 'to trace [*tracer*]' must also be understood in its contemporary slang meaning in French. '*Tracer*' in this sense means to move so quickly that one can only be apprehended by the traces of one's disappearance. Tracing leaves a line in place: a cinematic thread beyond which the motion 'follows itself' in the hope of never catching up to itself. Michaux meditated on the line on several occasions, in "Aventures de lignes," in "Lignes," and in *Émergences-Résurgences*.[20] The first text is a homage to Klee, to whom Michaux attributes his awakening to painting. Among other things, Michaux finds in Klee the freedom of a line that is "intransitive" in a certain sense, the result of an "inception of muscle" that prevents itself from arriving. Michaux would continue to recognize himself in this freedom:

> Like me, the line is seeking without knowing what it is seeking, it rejects what comes too easily, solutions offered, first temptations. Preventing itself from 'arriving,' line of blind investigation. Without leading to anything, without attempting to be beautiful or interesting, criss-crossing itself without turning a hair, without turning away, without turning itself in knots or knotting itself to something, without perceiving object, landscape, figure.
> Colliding with nothing, somnambulant line.
> Curved in places, yet not enlacing
> Encircling nothing and never encircled
> A line that has not yet made its choice, not ready to be finalized. Without preference, without accentuation, without completely giving in to appearances.
> … Watchful, wandering. Celibate line, it intends to remain so, does not submit, blind to the material world.
> It neither dominates, nor accompanies, and is certainly not subordinate.[21]

In his "Esquisses pédagogiques" (1925),[22] Klee began by evoking an "*active* line, frolicking freely. A promenade for the sake of promenading, without a particular goal." This line is clearly related to Michaux's lines to come, but in an abstract way; its activity is purely spatial, caught in a play of purely spatial forces (thus its resistance to creating a plane that would threaten its "passivation").

Michaux imagines a line that belongs to nothing, "without filiation," infinitely unwinding the skein of the 'ball.' The line transforms the inertia of the 'ball' into a tenuous activity. It gives birth to what Michaux calls, in a text from *Moments*, "the thin man":

> Little and lacunary
> in a hurry and knowing that quickly he has to know
> in his cockpit in his little galaxy
> on guard ...
> a pilot
> pilot as long as he can
> pilot or nothing[23]

Here, by means of 'tracing,' the subject is transformed into a "thin man," "all-purpose," or, again, an "airline pilot." Why a "pilot"? Because it is necessary to be wary of whatever pitfalls may await the line. Because the line could succeed too well, unravel to infinity, to the point where it becomes no more than the elimination of any plane, any thickness, and, in the end, of any tracing. Michaux experienced the horror of this becoming-line in a particularly difficult mescaline state:

> The main horror of it was that I was only a line. In normal life, you're a sphere, a sphere that comes upon panoramas ... . Here only a line. A line breaking into a thousand aberrations ... [24]

In the absence of dimension the pure line encloses even more than the 'ball.' And if the line "does not arrive," it is for the wrong reasons: it is because it never left, or because it left without finding any space in which to be. The line that should have been the pure affirmation of acting is now only the shape of pure submission without perspective, of an internal linearization in which it finds itself, as if removed from itself. But the other danger awaiting the line is enclosure, arrest. It is the opposite danger of a line that would arrive too well or too quickly. In a short text from 1983 devoted to children's drawings,[25] Michaux comments that the child really begins to draw only once he has broken the repetition of circling lines that constitutes a phase of his scribbling, once he has broken free of his "itch to include." In the beginning is repetition and the sphere. One day, however:

> One day after many days, escaping from the Bacchic round, a curved line will not go around as expected: it slows down and stops, a certain line of a surprised child, it means something to him, keeps him in suspense and makes him hold back and ponder.[26]

The child is on the road to resemblance. But 'resemblance,' as understood by Michaux, breaks with the outline. It has nothing to do with either the shading or the finish of the drawing. It begins with the incompletion of the outline, the opening of the sphere. 'Resemblance' is the polar opposite of a pictorial academicism that attempts to produce a surface, a hard and impenetrable crust. It is a purely physiognomic resemblance. The line, in order truly to grasp something of the world, must be prevented from closing up, enclosing. It must be contented with this allusive bending.

The line must be piloted 'celibately,' without wedding itself to any of its risks, equidistant from infinite fraying and arrested outline, from abstraction and the delimiting of the closed surface. In this space between, there is room for a rich variety of lines. In "Aventures de lignes," which was inspired by Klee, but in which Michaux was also thinking very much about himself, he catalogued families of lines. Unlike Klee, in "Esquisses pédagogiques" he did not limit himself to the trilogy of "active" lines (strolling or subject to delays), "intermediary" lines (half-way between the motion of a point and the effect of a plane), and "passive" lines (which compose a plane). He distinguished "traveling" lines, which "don't create objects so much as they create journeys, itineraries," "penetrating" lines, which "far from volume, far from centers, seek a center nonetheless, a center that is less apparent, but is more the master of the mechanism," "allusive" lines, "mad about enumerating ... creating microscopic palaces of proliferating cellular life."

And yet this space between is risky and perhaps impossible. First and foremost because, in plastic reality, the only way for a line to exist spatially is to give itself up. Its true freedom to exist lies entirely in this negation by which it interrupts itself, in order to come out of abstraction and become a *stroke*. The tracing adopts the line's power of affirmation, but only finds its consistency in the negation that brings it to a halt. The stroke cannot have the power to cross out something else, and, in particular, another stroke, unless it is first intrinsically an affirmation–negation, an enacted yes–no. And, in this way, it is faithful to the ambivalent nature of vision as Michaux describes it in *Saisir*:

> As for the vision of things and beings, one sees by excluding as much as by receiving.
> *There are no innocent gazes.*[27]

And, therefore, there are no innocent forms. Behind every form, and in order for it to be possible, lies its obligation to disobey itself ("as if, as a child, I had sworn it to myself," Michaux writes). The disobedience of the line is called the 'stroke.' One of Michaux's last published collections is thus entitled *Par des traits* [By Strokes]. It is more visual than verbal, since it is essentially composed of tracings. The drawing in it is hard, utterly black on a white background, without the slightest nuance from wash. And if the stroke appears here very close to the sign, on the road to semiotization, it is not because it adopts an ideogrammatic appearance as it does elsewhere. Rather, it is because it overexposes the ambivalence of the stroke, its dual logical power of affirmation and negation.

Once this ambivalence has been recognized it becomes Michaux's principal building-block, not only in the construction of himself (recall his statement that became the title of Claude Lefort's wonderful study: "I built myself upon an absent column"), but also in the construction of all representation. He recognizes it at work in *Saisir*, a book of texts and drawings collected in a kind of representative "predacity": in this work, Michaux wanted to open himself "to the beings of the world that see each other," to appropriate a kind of personal bestiary by means of graphic signs. But the painter-predator met with some bizarre resistance along the way:

> The animals, subjected chaotically to my contradictory representation, were crossed by brusque strokes that were like great negations. Which they really were.[28]

But these negating strokes are also constructive. In drawing, it is even *with* negation that one best represents. And this explains, paradoxically perhaps, why the most domesticated or the most familiar animals (dogs, cats, sparrows, and horses—animals that are too submissive, too similar, or too close to human) are absent from *Saisir*, whereas loathsome, repulsive insects crowd the work, as if they had been captured by the negativity of the stroke. The stroke that crosses out is their architecture.

The ambivalence of the gesture thus moves into the stroke. The stroke implies this ambivalence intrinsically. But it is also liable to spread beyond the stroke, to distribute itself among the different elements of painting, thereby enriching the pictorial field without abdicating any of its representative tension. I am thinking specifically of all the processes that use the conflict of different materials as a constructive force. This is, for example, what Michaux does with watercolor, using the water as an agent to dissolve stroke and color:

> I hurl water to attack the pigments, which undo themselves, contradict each other, intensify, or become their opposite, jeering at the forms and lines that have been sketched, making a mockery of all fixity, all drawing, brother and sister of my state that no longer sees anything remaining standing.[29]

Watercolor is the height of triumph through failure. It opposes the positive affirmation of the line to its dissolution by the water that soaks up contours and colors. The drawing is subjected to water's own autonomous time, a time of liquefaction and incompletion. And yet Michaux reclaims this cinematic power to revive forms, both which he provokes and to which he submits, as a faithfulness to form and to himself, to his own unfixable state. His most violent watercolors are from the dark period when his wife was dying in 1948, and they pile on every negating gesture. Returning from the hospital, he would rush to the watercolored paper, bringing together the interruption of the stroke, the attack of the fixity with water, and finally the perforation of paper as if it were another skin to be made to bleed:

> In pen, furiously scratching out, I slash at surfaces to work devastation upon them, as devastation the entire day has been lived out in me, making of my being a sore. May this paper, also, be as a sore![30]

This is no doubt painting's ultimate thrust: the interruption of the stroke, the dissolution of the form, the piercing of the paper. The farthest limit, where everything runs the risk of disappearing, even the wound itself.

Repelling

Michaux also experienced other starting points, or "inceptions," one of which was the exact opposite of drawing and watercolor. It wasn't until 1954 that, already at ease with Indian ink, he abandoned the brush and poured the ink directly onto the paper. What is of utmost importance here is the random way the ink spreads. The spilled ink creates an urgent situation: it demands an intervention in the short time it takes to dry (and not, like watercolor, in the time it takes to be absorbed by the paper):

> This dirty black flow that sprawls out, demolishing the page and its horizon, which it crosses blindly, stupidly, unbearably, obliging me to intervene.
>
> From the fits of anger it provokes in me, I recover, I return to it, divide it, quarter it, send it packing. I want nothing to do with that naturally slobbering blot, I reject it, undo it, scatter it. It's my turn!
>
> The sweeping gestures I make to get rid of the puddles naturally help to express great disgust, great exasperation. They are expressive. I have to work quickly. The somber pseudopods that soon emerge from the blots swollen with ink *summon me to see clearly immediately*, to decide instantly.
>
> As I struggle with the blot, there are battles.
>
> I repel it.[31]

This practice brings a certain number of reversals into play. Representation no longer arises from a positive movement that discovers its negativity along the way. It occurs entirely as a response to the negativity of the "dirty black flow" that must be made positive again. The initiative no longer belongs to the ball and its "inceptions of muscles"; now it is the blot, mirror-like, that causes its "somber pseudopods" to emerge. The action required is no longer one of intervention, but of response. The time of urgency begun by the spread liquid is no longer, as it was with watercolor, a passive time in which the medium imposes its duration of dissolution on the painter's propositions. It is an overactive time. The spread black ink beckons the painter to "see clearly," that is, to invert its sign; it forces an awakening. It creates a state of panic, reviving other anxieties of failure:

> Panic, then, on seeing the paper soak up too quickly, or the blob turn me away from my purpose, that panic is almost immediately echoed in me by a thousand other moments of panic, called up from my not too happy past.[32]

But this panic, objectified on the page, becomes an instrument of painting, a stimulus to combat, a dynamic of opposition. The painter's gesture no longer consists of *tracing*, but of *repelling* an invasive material. From now on, form is asserted as a hollow. Its positivity is in the negation of a negation.

Revealing

What has also been up-ended, as in a game of *Gestalt*, is the relation of precession between background and figure. The initiative of drawing was one in which the figure asserted itself before the background, undermining any effects of surface, of closure. Watercolor began the process of reversal. It transformed the paper into a mirror, not because it gleamed like a mirror but because it returned the initiative to the background, thereby transforming the paper into a space where figures were revealed, set free. From then on a Narcissus, Protean and anxious, could be mirrored in the black reflections (black is his 'crystal ball') and see not just one figure emerge, but a thousand, unrecognizable and fleeting. The spilled ink leads us not only to the contradictory gestures of repelling but also to a space of apparition. It forms the dynamic version of the *dessins à fond noir* (the black backgrounds) from 1936–37. After this time, Michaux drew from it an effect of depth and emergence:

> As soon as I begin, as soon as a few colors have been set on the sheet of black paper, it ceases to be paper, and becomes night. The colors put down at random have become apparitions emerging from the night.
> I come to blackness. Blackness brings me back to bedrock, to origin.
> Seat of deep feelings. From the night comes the unexplained, the unparticularized, the unattached to visible causes, the surprise attack, mystery, the sense of the sacred, fear … and monsters, begotten of the void, not of a mother.[33]

It is not, therefore, the blackness that creates depth—it is the color, set down ahead of it, that hollows it out and transforms it into a space of paradoxical generation. The black is "made night" by the color. Its neutrality is transmuted into an active and productive negativity. Color and night are jointly rent from one another. There is here a somber miracle that brings us back to the question of birth, or rather, to its avoidance. The black background causes apparitions to emerge from 'nothing,' but in this it is akin to the creating subject's desire for self-sufficiency, for the subject also dreams of being born from nothing. This non-matricial space offers to its creator ghost-like apparitions that are unstable and

195

without ontological consistency, but he recognizes himself in this very deficiency. The black background, before the ink, thus acts as a kind of developer, revealing latent images. It transforms each figure into an image that has arisen from a latency; it mimics the subject's inner life, mysterious and unfathomable to himself. Other devices later played this same role. From 1944 to 1947, it was the *frottages* that seemed to bring out eloquent figures through the hazards of the medium. In the space of developing/revealing, nothing is truly to be created, and everything is to be revealed, set free. Black here has no pedagogical or illustrative value, and revelation can take place on any background, light or dark, as long as it is examined as a space of/for emergence.

What, then, does this subject see in the paper? It sees 'figures' rising, 'figures' which we must understand here as 'faces.' But these faces don't resemble the immobile mask of the finished man. Incomplete and fluctuating, they aggressively defy simple resemblance:

> Behind the set features, desperately seeking a way out, expressions like a pack of howling dogs. From the brush, in black blobs, somehow they flow forth: they liberate themselves …
> The first few times, one is surprised.
> Faces of lost souls, of criminals, sometimes, neither known nor absolutely unfamiliar either (strange, remote correspondence!) … . Faces of sacrificed personalities, 'selves' that life, determination, ambition, a propensity for rectitude and consistency, stifled, killed off.[34]

From the night of the paper all the selves emerge, or rather all the phases, all the moments of the self that had to be denied in order to be, but for all that have not been reduced to nothing. They continue to haunt subjectivity. They bear the stigma of this negation and emerge as a flow of tormented faces, distraught or full of hatred.

Painting has the power to unset the mask of the self, to revive in paper all its *frères maudits* and to summon them back from the night into which they were rejected. Similarly, other uninhibiting experiences had caused these repressed 'selves' to emerge from the subject's own face: during a mescaline-induced state recounted in *Misérable miracle*, Michaux saw the face of an "enraged madman," "set to kill" in the mirror. But this proximity was experienced as infinitely dangerous, bordering on insanity. No screen of paper could provide shelter from this other self, the madman in himself. "Infinite crowd: our clan," wrote Michaux. Painting provides this wandering crowd with a face and a place. Without lingering over it: cinematically, one could say. We recall Michaux's advice:

> The mirror is not the place to observe yourself. Men,
> look at yourselves in the paper.[35]

We now have a better idea of the *genealogy* of Michaux's pictorial gestures. These gestures struggle against a dual inertia: first, that of a badly-born body (fetal state, sainthood, sleepiness, fatigue) that seeks a path to escape from itself, to produce itself in movement (these will be the dynamic and affirmative routes of tracing, but also the reactive routes of repelling), and second, that of a self that is born too well, fixed in its masks, and deaf to the world of impulses and virtual existences that continuously reside in it. The pictorial gestures make birth go back into labor by means of all the forms of revelation that cause latent figures to arise from the background. These gestures fight faces with faces. Painting, the visible output of which is nothing but cooled traces, is thus a potential mobility that allows one to go back in time, within the images of the self, to the moment when they are still hesitating to form themselves. This potential is itself faceless, and it tirelessly connects a wholly unfigurable origin to the parade of faces in which it could have embodied itself.

Although the imagination's activity here may appear unrelated to what has always been Michaux's explicit pictorial project—the elaboration of a graphic language, or rather of "emotions in signs that only distress and humor can decipher"—it is in fact from this unattainable genesis of the self that Michaux draws all his semantic resources. There is not a single pictorial gesture that does not find its urgency or its resonance in the subject's attempt to be. If we compare Michaux to those modernists contemporary with the early part of his career, we can more easily see what distinguishes him from them. Kandinsky's concerns may appear related to Michaux's when the former attempts, in his theoretical writings, to elaborate an alphabet of forms, especially since he deals with forms that are always perceived in their energetic dimension: "In fact, it is not external forms that define the content of a pictorial work, but rather, the forces and tensions that reside in these forms".[36]

For Kandinsky, however, the work is elaborated by the accumulation of elementary forms, each one endowed with its own tension and entering into composition with the others in order to compose a global energetic configuration. If we relate this plastic approach to the construction of a language, we must understand it as being *semiotic* in nature, composing a whole from the value of each individual element.[37] Michaux took the opposite approach. He broke completely with the 'alphabetic' temptations of his early works. He in fact proceeded not by signs, but by elementary semantic operations of affirmation, negation, or affirmation-negation. The gesture, more than the form, is engaged from the outset in a discursive creation of meaning. And as we have seen, these semantic operations are never abstract. They are altogether psychologically motivated. They go back to paths that are impulse-driven, "motion" driven, paths that create the self somewhere between being and the refusal to be, between opening and closing. They take them up, prolong them, place them in dialogue with one another, and reelaborate them. The forms produced in this way may thus be characterized as 'emotions in signs'; this is how they 'speak to the mood.' The myth of the 'ball,' begun in the "Portrait of A.," goes well beyond Michaux's own case; it bears within it a certain universality. It speaks to us of the most archaic movements that are at the origin of every self. Still, we would be betraying Michaux's work were we to reduce it merely to this psychological expressiveness. If, indeed, his work draws its productive energy from it, it is not limited to it. Michaux of course encounters forms (obviously: he is a painter), but they are secondary to his gestures. There is no traced movement that does not overflow beyond its 'motion' in order to confront the one who has traced it with a stubborn externality that cannot be reduced to its origin as drive. This is true of even the simplest stroke, the individuation of which always exceeds intention, surprising us, making us think. And it is obviously this return of form that Michaux was attempting to consider in its pure state, by blindly spilling ink (or water) on paper—beginning, in a sense, by the 'return.' And then the question of expression is reversed: it is by responding to what form proposes that the painter invents himself, and these proposals are also "psychological sites,"[38] seductive or frightening, uninhabitable even: proposals that are unceasingly accepted, rejected, modified, without our ever being able to tire of their miraculous profusion.

197

NOTES

1. Henri Michaux, *Idéogrammes en Chine*, Montpellier (Fata Morgana) 1975.

2. *Par des traits* 1984.

3. Wassily Kandinsky, *Du spirituel dans l'art*, Paris (Folio-Essais) 1989, p. 116. This is the French translation of *Uber das Geistige in der Kunst* (1912).

4. Wassily Kandinsky, *Point et ligne sur plan*, Paris (Folio-Essais) 1991; first published 1926. This is the French translation of *Punkt und Linie zu Flache*, Munich (Albert Langen) *c.* 1926.

5. Henri Michaux, "Spiritualisme," *Le Disque vert*, January 1925, reprinted in *Œuvres complètes*, I, Paris (Bibliothèque de la Pléiade, Gallimard) 1998, pp. 58–61.

6. Max Morise, "Les Yeux enchantés," *La Révolution surréaliste*, no. 1, 1 December 1924, p. 16.

7. André Masson, "Propos sur le surréalisme," *Méditations*, no. 3, autumn 1961; reprinted in *Le Rebelle du surréalisme*, Paris (Hermann) 1994, p. 41. (All translations are mine unless otherwise specified—Trans.)

8. Reproduced in Alfred Pacquement, *Henri Michaux. Peintures*, Paris (Gallimard) 1983, p. 160.

9. Max Ernst, "Comment on force l'inspiration," *Le SASDLR*, 6, May 1933, p. 43.

10. Ernst briefly used the term "fantomism" to designate the effect produced by these techniques. Klee also painted on a black background. See, for example, his *Black Prince* of 1927, to which Michaux makes reference ten years later in his *Prince de la nuit* (Prince of the Night).

11. And often reprinted since. See, for example, Raymond Bellour (ed.), *Henri Michaux*, Paris (Éditions de l'Herne) 1966.

12. Henri Michaux, *Selected Writings*, trans. Richard Ellman, New York (New Directions) 1968, pp. ix–x.

13. *Œuvres complètes*, I, 1998, p. 609.

14. *Ibid.*

15. *Ibid.*, p. 613.

16. *Passages* 1963, p. 74.

17. I am thinking, for example, of "Le Sportif au lit," in *La Nuit remue* (1935), in *Œuvres complètes*, I, 1998, p. 426.

18. Henri Michaux, *Mouvements*, Paris (Collection Le Point du Jour, Gallimard) 1951; trans. Michael Fineberg in Guggenheim/Pompidou 1978, p. 71. Cited in the text hereafter as Fineberg in Guggenheim/Pompidou 1978, followed by page number.

19. Henri Michaux, *Faces aux verrous*, Paris (Gallimard) 1967, p. 29; first published 1934.

20. *Émergences-Résurgences* 1972.

21. *Émergences-Résurgences* 1972, p. 12.

22. Reprinted in *Théorie de l'art moderne*, Paris (Folio-Essais) 1998, p. 73.

23. Ball 1994, pp. 233–34.

24. *Ibid.*, p. 204.

25. Henri Michaux, *Les Commencements*, Montpellier (Fata Morgana) 1983.

26. *Ibid.*, p. 12.

27. Henri Michaux, *Saisir*, Montpellier (Fata Morgana) 1979, unpaginated.

28. *Ibid.*, unpaginated.

29. *Émergences-Résurgences* 1972, p. 40.

30. *Ibid.*, p. 36; Fineberg in Guggenheim/Pompidou 1978, p. 60.

31. *Émergences-Résurgences* 1972, p. 59.

32. *Passages* 1963, p. 99; Fineberg in Guggenheim/Pompidou 1978, p. 43.

33. *Émergences-Résurgences* 1972, p. 26; Fineberg in Guggenheim/Pompidou 1978, p. 38 (trans. modified).

34. Henri Michaux, "En pensant au phénomène de la peinture," (1946), reprinted in *Passages* 1963, p. 88; translated in Fineberg in Guggenheim/Pompidou 1978, p. 43.

35. Ball 1994, p. 312.

36. Kandinsky 1991, p. 36.

37. This kind of composition is characteristic of Kandinsky's painting, and is especially noticeable in a work like *Small Dream in Red* (1925), which can be considered a perfect illustration of this theory.

38. I have borrowed this wonderful expression from Henri Focillon's *La Vie des formes*, Paris (PUF) 1996, p. 23; first published 1943. Focillon writes, regarding Doric art and its transfiguration of the Greek landscape: "the life of forms defines psychological sites, without which the genius of certain environments would be opaque and incomprehensible for everyone who is a part of them."

THE UTOPIA OF THE SIGN

Raymond Bellour

IN MICHAUX THERE IS A TRUE UTOPIAN LINE—the only one actively to fulfill the mad cravings for temporal and spatial mutations that his intolerance of reality inspired. It is the utopia of the sign.

Very early on, Michaux learnt languages, languages other than his native Walloon. First Flemish, between the ages of seven and about eleven or twelve, "my second language, which I spoke as well if not better than French—since forgotten."[1] Then Latin, which he pursued with the help of his father—"a beautiful language, one that sets him apart from others, transplants him: his first departure."[2] Then, in the mid-1920s, when he had settled in Paris, one sees him turning to new languages and speaking of this to his various correspondents. Thus he wrote his friend Robert Guiette, "I'm incredibly tired, overworked, and am determined to work myself harder and harder. I'm taking lessons in Annamese, Spanish, English, I'm drawing, I'm writing."[3] The same day, he asked Claude Cahun, with whom he was for a short time closely linked, and who in those years gave him English lessons, to procure for him *Annamese in 30 Lessons* at Albin Michel, 22 rue Huyghens.[4] Michaux furthermore wrote Paulhan: "Right now my only interests are alphabets and languages, especially Annamese. I can make all forty-three of its sounds, which none but the initiated are able to tell apart."[5]

From this movement, where writing, drawing, and language intermingle, suddenly there appeared two examples of a writer modestly venturing into painting and drawing—works which embody a power of enigma it would take Michaux a lifetime to unfold towards ever-greater incandescence. Both of these ink compositions are dated October 1927.[6] The first of them, presented to Jean Paulhan as an "*essai d'écriture*," is called *Alphabet*. It consists of signs neatly arrayed into several blocks. At first mimicking a script which might seem born of very ancient times, the bottom lines widen out and signs become fewer and farther between, better exposing their contrived aspect as well as their ambiguous suggestions of figuration. The second study is entitled *Narration*. It, too, constitutes a block of writing, from top to bottom one that is narrower on the page. Here, by contrast, hazy and spread-out signs draw closer together towards the bottom of the page, forming compact lines that are like pieces of thread or vermicelli. The connection between these two titles, in its very simplicity, is stunning. The sign, then, is also given over to fiction, obeying the strange law without law which dictates that it should contrive *itself*, like the language it embodies, and thus represent itself as the image of its own enigma.

This is what Michaux was dreaming about, some years later and in a different fashion, when he came to grips with China. His spontaneous eagerness for fiction, which would be forever in conflict with his wish for supreme harmony, was at this point shelved in favor of a combined meditation on Chinese painting, theater, writing, and poetry.[7] Things crop up in a very scrambled way on these pages, making them rather tricky to comment upon. But this much, at least, may be gathered from them: Chinese culture is the product of reductions at once elliptical and manifest, a system of deductive allusions by which nature and code echo one another, perpetually and patiently making signals, so to speak, to each other. From this point on, Michaux would forever endeavor ideally to transpose this state of affairs into his own writing-painting needs, in order to compensate for the distress bound up with the all-pervasive subjectivity of the West, which he named, in connection with love and in contrast with that displayed by the Chinese woman, "white anxiety."[8]

The most distinct token of all this was destined to remain sheerly virtual (this is, after all, the law of utopias). In 1938, while *Plume précédé de lointain intérieur* was once more taking shape around the only hero who appeared to offer Michaux a sustained guarantee of fiction,[9] he announced within the book, among the list of works by its author, the following project "in preparation": "The rudiments of a universal ideographic language containing nine hundred ideograms and a grammar." This is the sole mention ever made of a plan so specific. Two features may be deduced from this description: on the one hand, the rudimentary and thus restricted nature of this language, indicated by the small number of ideograms envisaged; on the other hand, and on the contrary, its universal nature. This is the path that takes off from and goes beyond "Chinese, which could have been a universal language."[10] This is the dream of the impossible, a language contrived or mimicked by just one man, and nevertheless belonging to a community.

At one point, Michaux seemed to adapt this project of his within the conception of his imaginary voyages: in the fiction of "The Dialect of the *Oudemaïs*," in *Ici, Poddema*. But in the first instance, this language was in no way ideographic; so as a species of language it falls short of the sign, remaining purely phonic. What's more, Michaux limited examples of it to about twelve words. Last, but not least, it was a delirious language, in the sense that its few outlined principles were designed to warp, contradict, or disregard one another, and above all to produce, one by one and as a group, a logical vertigo. Still, ever a gambling man and ever committed to this dream, Michaux conserved a link between this dialect, as false as it is fantastic, and Chinese the way he imagined it to be. "And what is *Hag*, present in almost every sentence?/ It's the uncertainty syllable."[11] Of the Chinese language, of its short, one-syllable words, Michaux said that "the syllable echoes with uncertainty," that often "a flooding consonant (*n* or *g*) submerges it in the sound of a gong."[12]

Above and beyond this mirror play, it was in *Mouvements*, in 1951, that the project he had envisaged was given a real semblance of execution. The book's Postface, which accompanies the poem and sixty-four pages of drawings, sets out to establish their nature and relations.[13] Michaux directly refers to the drawings in question as "signs." He has filled twelve hundred pages with them, he admits, from which, thanks to René Bertelé, he made the selection in the book (if one goes by a very loose average of ten signs per page, that comes out to be around twelve thousand signs or figures—Michaux mentions a certain day on which he supposedly did nearly five thousand of them). He clarifies the circumstances of their genesis:

I had been urged to go back to composing ideograms, which I had been doing on and off for twenty years and the pursuit of which seems indeed to be part of my destiny, but only as a lure and a fascination. Over and over again I had abandoned them for lack of any success. I tried once more, but gradually the forms 'in movement' supplanted the constructed forms, the consciously composed characters. Why? I enjoyed doing them more. Their movement became my movement.

A pure graphic thrust, an expressive language of the body thus takes the place of any utopian refiguration of language's code or of any other set system, to which, nevertheless, the word "signs" still bears witness. Thus, in the poem *Mouvements*, the final apostrophe to "signs"—the term there standing, in a meaningful way, for "blots" and "gestures"—finds itself precisely and emphatically split in the name of two postulations. Rather than naming and arranging the world by referring to its reality, the sign must allow one simultaneously to dodge the "trap of other people's language" and to devise "at last a direct writing for the unwinding of forms."[14] Thus, in the Postface to the poem, Michaux firmly pits the traces of drawing, a "new language," an "unhoped-for writing," against the "verbal," against words— which are enemies as much for being words as for being "other people's words."

And yet, barely three years later, while the poem *Mouvements* was being reissued on its own in *Face aux verrous*, Michaux published a text in which the return to his former utopia has recourse to the very word that had just been used to move away from it: "Signs."[15] Michaux starts off again on the basis of that which *Mouvements* had firmly ruled out: reality, knowledge, and totality. "All of nature is signs, signs upon signs, a macle of signs". He then likens the mask ("*a single principal sign*") to the pictographic sign because of their admirable rigidity, and opposes the resonant liquidity of words to "clear-cut signs of which one is the mechanic, not the violinist."[16] Inspired by the sciences, Michaux briefly dreams of a language in tune with "this hard century," this "age of engineers," a "totally contructed" new language, "a tool composed of signs," destined to disclose "a new intelligence." From there, he moves seamlessly into painting, in which, strangely, "signs appear. Certainly not to create a universal language and, in fact, we're not even sure that they are indeed signs." Even so, the term stuck, informing the discussions of Capogrossi and (somewhat more ironically) Mathieu, as well as Michaux's comments on his *own* signs. "But were they signs? They were gestures … They were movements (unfortunate limit). Later I broke the movements down into bits./ Maybe all of this was a way of running away from the sign." Thus, towards the end of this text, a utopian line forms anew around the values of stability and, via that, of the social exchange of signs. Michaux presents the equivocal notion of "situation-sign" to designate that which he has not, as he adds, "even begun to find." Cannily reintroducing the idea of nature, he concludes with words that recall, in a much softer tone, the fervent anticipations of the poem "Avenir," written sixteen years earlier:[17] "What an experience it will be when the time is ripe at last and, having got into the habit of thinking in signs, we are able to exchange secrets with a few natural strokes like a handful of twigs."

Twenty-five, thirty years later, shortly before Michaux's death, the line thus opened up led straight to two small books that closely complement one another, *Saisir* and *Par des traits*.[18] Blending words with images (either on the page itself or in separate notebooks, as had been the case in *Mouvements*), these two books mainly renewed a tension between language and non-language, stability and motion, codification and freedom, social utopia and subjective withdrawal. The sign scurries over the space of this tension like a panic-stricken insect. Many insects are scrawled on the pages of *Saisir*, linked to his umpteenth attempt at abecedarium, a bestiary, or a graphic dictionary. Michaux was off again, sliding from represented reality, the likeness of which he always refused in the end, to the gesture of execution itself, which he called "*abstract* execution." In this way, this first text extended the power of sign towards perceptible abstraction. The sign became virtually capable of treating not just animals, men, or gestures, but 'situations,' that is, concrete, everyday wholes, at once ordinary and fantastic (Michaux, multiplying the equivocal relations between reality, code, sound, and meaning, put it remarkably: "language itself, its depth"). But this, by the same token, was in order to confer upon the ideogram or pictogram, above and beyond their indomitable fixedness, a motion, "a special impetus." A final example illustrates this chimerical desire to seize, to "translate" the most abstract fundamentals (with the following unresolved question —"Is there anything that can escape signs altogether?"). A discussion heard on the radio about the composition of matter and the birth of the universe immediately modified the various drawings, lines, and signs, already under way for several months (almost as if the book were "live")—and the last drawings of the volume, stratigraphic, pointillist, immediately bear proof of this change: "With a small, leaning structure in the air, I graduated to the thrilling, noble, and great adventure that is the elucidation of the universe as a whole."

Par des traits, on the other hand, puts the emphasis on the idea of pre-language: "unfinished languages," "bits of languages" that have yielded before the tyranny of "languages of implementation, of management." These pre-languages have four characteristics (which are, deliberately, somewhat indistinguishable from each other). They remain figurative, pictographic, and ideographic. They are impoverished, made of few words (in contrast to overly rich languages, recorded in the account books of the "offices of Universal Science"). They are playful, daring ("recreational signs, marks on a tree trunk that the straining bark eradicated without anyone intending it"). They are local, and in the minority ("languages of very limited means … language for limited needs, among friends, not territorial"). From this *bricolage*, from these singular, inventive, and minute "*rapprochements*," literature and poems turn things to their advantage, a "new magical power" taking over "these bridges leading from lines to things, to gestures, to situations" (via analogies, similes, and metaphors). Thus, confronted with languages everywhere "catalogued, all of them restrictive," this force is able to stay within sight of "*a more modest, more intimate language*," which, even so, will be "not really a language, but a thing very much alive, more like emotions in signs … Signs that would enable us to be open to the world differently, creating and developing *a different function* in man, DISALIENATING HIM."

Thus, from the handful of twigs to the marks on tree bark, from dreamt-of dictionaries to the seizure of situations as abstract as they are alive, one can see the conflicting utopia outlined in "Signes" and beyond, for so long, in various forms, as it reformulates itself. The point is that literature, or rather, the activity of writing, however Michaux may have disowned it (the section of *Par des traits* in which this movement sets itself up is entitled "Of Language and Writing/ Why the urge to turn away from them"), remains within the very utopia that would have it transformed into "emotions in signs"—just as, in *Mouvements*, in order to arrive at this direct writing that allows the "unwinding of forms," one must open oneself up to those signs that allow one to "rediscover the gift of languages," and thus gain access to one's *own* language. This unresolved, unresolvable tension is clearly utopia itself. That is, above all, as these books, *Mouvements*, *Saisir*, *Par des traits*, and many others show as much as tell: the sign, the idea of sign, embodies the spiraling vanishing line that joins, in a single divided gesture, the impossible fusion of writing and painting-drawing.[19] The sign is thus the instrumental and theoretical locus of those passages informing the crux of this *œuvre*, altogether unique for being so fully both one and double.

One may somewhat concretize this whirlwind of thought and affect by relating a circumstance surrounding the composition of *Idéogrammes en Chine*.[20] In 1969, more than forty years after his study of the Annamese language, mentioned in a few of his letters, and just under four decades after his single, long trip to China, Michaux took up Chinese. A notebook attests to this,[21] mentioning, without any other explanations, at least four sessions between November 27 and December 1. Michaux copied out, over thirty-seven pages, various sequences of ideograms, complete with explanatory comments, using a textbook written in English and designed for people studying Japanese, or more precisely, for people learning the simple Chinese characters (ideograms and pictograms) used in Japanese. What's more, the Michaux archives contain a linguaphone with a Chinese workbook and records. While no indication of date is given, the device must be from this same period. One is first struck by the fact that so late in life Michaux set about this exercise in a very speculative fashion, perhaps to prepare himself for the preface he would soon write for *La Calligraphie chinoise*. Curious above all about how things work, keeping a constant lookout for a knowledge that his text would transpose according to its own objectives, he sought to essay the line, the trace, by following, wherever the examples took him, the graphic evolution of the characters. And yet, it is remarkable how this exercise in copying reveals a noticeable clumsiness, and even a flagrant carelessness in his tracing of a good number of strokes.[22] One might conclude that he may have been writing on his lap, with no firm support to lean on. But this would still not explain everything—for example, his strokes that slant when they should be vertical. It is more interesting to suppose that Michaux was here demonstrating a particular incompetence in copying, both when the character is a rather good likeness (as Chinese characters were in the beginning) and when it is more abstract (as they have subsequently become). For copying, with its obligatory realism linking it back to the model, absolutely curbs every single profound motion of the body, every instinct of the hand executing this motion. Just as Michaux was rarely able to copy a text without distorting it or somehow rewriting it, so he subjected characters to a disfigurement that at times causes them to lose even their very meaning.

Towards its close, this notebook displays seven pages of drawings of a totally different kind. They are for the most part minute, more or less realistic sketches: a bird on the branch of a tree; a man's head in a landscape, near a house; faces; a cat; *etc.* The drawings are so poor that one has trouble believing that they were born of Michaux's hand. But by what other hand could they have been traced, located on a page where one reads words written in his handwriting, however unrelated they may be to these hints at representation? Here too, it is more interesting to suppose that Michaux's profound unfitness for copying was the reason behind this disconcerting end-product. In either case, it was the sign as code, as code of knowledge and recognition, that was being aimed at—and more or less abjectly obeyed, and yet ruined. And it was precisely in the gap between the conventional sign of language and the analogical sign of representation that Michaux set out expressively to refigure the sign, both written and graphic—the written sign attempting, in spite of the constantly denounced burdens and inevitabilities of language, to speak of the graphic sign, which is deployed and re-deployed to nurture the mad hope for a single 'language' made up of both, a language of signs that would be at once personal and social, born of the absolute specificity of the body and yet designed for exchange, a language for all, yet appropriate to just a few. These conflicting utopian drives inform Michaux's dual vision of the ever-exemplary Chinese language in *Idéogrammes en Chine*—a vision that construes Chinese as being constantly in evolution, constantly in regression.[23]

One day in 1966, in the course of one of his rare interviews, entitled "The Experience of Signs," Michaux spoke more directly than ever before about his grand project.

> I dreamed for a time, without any serious results, of searching for a universal language. I tried to come up with characters clear for all, independent of speech. But nothing ever came of it … Or if it did, one character was never different enough from the next. I was missing the point. In Chinese writing, when the pen was in use before the brush, anyone could understand the characters in a second. I've always hoped to find this language among other peoples or in other places, in Africa, for example, but let's admit that this is never too clear or that it remains conventional: man, woman, mountain, stream, nothing more. It's a hope that I have not fulfilled. I would willingly give all that I have to achieve this.
>
> I wanted to do this research in a team, but I could never find anyone but oddballs like myself. Still, I remain persuaded that there is something to be done in that direction. I wanted to sketch out characters with a psychic content. Human beings today are dissatisfied with their language. Beyond signals—signage—there will soon be five hundred signs necessary in today's world. At present the problem of signals and non-verbalizable signals is key. Graphic arts, in so many ways related to man, will grow richer and richer, more and more precise.
>
> All that I'm articulating here is simply my regret at having sensed a direction but having waited too long to begin.[24]

Another day, a wartime day, in Lavandou or Paris, Michaux perhaps came the nearest ever to the utopian point that impelled him along his way. He wrote "Alphabet," and conceived two pages of pen drawings opposite it:[25] thirty-seven signs or figures, distributed into boxes set up in a regular grid (with just the touch of irregularity that makes the order bearable: a few empty boxes, one sign for two boxes, three signs in one enormous box, two in one single box, a sign outside of a box). Most of these figures are creatures and animals, but also objects, lines, all more or less enigmatic. In this alphabet of essences animated by a strange motion, the line displays an amazing clumsiness, a mastery of childish naïveté. The text recounts, in the first person, the experience of a death and resurrection. The dying man casts one final glance on the creatures, so as to keep only their essence. "They dwindled, and at last were reduced to a sort of alphabet, but an alphabet that could have served in the other world, *in any world*." In this way the chill of death is defeated; the hero, soothed by this process, is able to climb back up "the open slope of life."

In the metamorphosis alluded to in this text, in the words chosen to do so, opposite the images illustrating it, and "without involving speech" (as he noted in his interview), there is something so precise that one might just discern the fullest, most all-embracing lines Michaux ever wrote, concerning his great dream. This was all that he ever sought: a sort of alphabet that could have served in the other world, *in any world*.

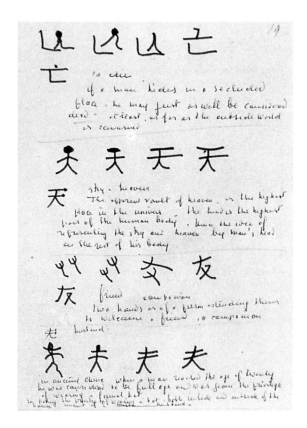

Two pages from Michaux's 1969 notebook, recording his study of Chinese calligraphy

NOTES

1. "Lettre-mémo" to René Bertelé, *Œuvres complètes*, I, 1998, p. 995.

2. "Some Information about Fifty-Nine Years of Existence," *Œuvres complètes*, I, 1998, p. cxxx.

3. Letter dating from April 30, 1925 (Archives and Museum of Literature, Brussels), *Œuvres complètes*, I, 1998, p. lxxxvii.

4. Private collection. *Ibid.*

5. IMEC. *Ibid.*

6. They can be found in Pacquement 1983, pp. 22–23.

7. *Un barbare en Asie*, *Œuvres complètes*, I, 1998, pp. 364–67.

8. *Ibid.*, p. 362.

9. *Un certain Plume* was published in 1930.

10. *Un barbare en Asie*, *Œuvres complètes*, I, 1998, p. 365.

11. *Ailleurs*, Paris (Gallimard) 1967, pp. 220–22 (*Ici, Poddema* was first published in 1945).

12. *Un barbare en Asie*, *Œuvres complètes*, I, 1998, p. 361. In Michaux, "gong" is one of the elected terms of the invocative, musical-poetic capacity (See "Le Gong fidèle d'un mot," *Ecuador*, *Œuvres complètes*, I, 1998, p. 162, as well as *La Nuit remue* and the poem "Je suis gong," *ibid.*, p. 505).

13. "Poésie/Gallimard," *Face aux verrous*, Paris (Gallimard) 1992 (1967), pp. 199–201.

14. *Ibid.*, pp. 18–19.

15. It was published in *XXème siècle*, no. 4, January 1954, pp. 48–50. The text is illustrated with three Indian ink drawings by Michaux, similar to the figures in *Mouvements*. Never republished in Michaux's lifetime, "Signes" was reissued in *Henri Michaux. Le langage du peintre le regard du poète*, exhib. cat., Paris, Galerie Thessa Herold, 1994, pp. 71–75. It will also appear in the second volume of *Œuvres complètes*.

16. He thus reverses, practically word for word, his almost contemporaneous longing for a music-language. See "Premières impressions," *Passages*, Paris (Gallimard) 1950.

17. *Œuvres complètes*, I, 1998, pp. 604–06, in *Plume précédé de Lointain intérieur*.

18. Published by Fata Morgana, Montpellier 1979, 1984; both are unpaginated.

19. Or, to put it like Foucault or Deleuze, between visible and pronounceable; Deleuze elaborated on this distinction in his work *Foucault*, Paris (Minuit) 1986, using *Les Mots et les choses* and especially Foucault's essay *Ceci n'est pas une pipe*, Montpellier (Fata Morgana) 1973.

20. *Idéogrammes en Chine*, Montpellier (Fata Morgana) 1975. The test was first published in 1971 as the preface to Léon Tchang Long-Yan's book, *La Calligraphie chinoise. Un art à quatre dimensions*, Paris (Club français du livre).

21. This forty-two-page spiral notebook was included in the sale of Maurice Saillet's library (no. 195, Drouot, March 15, 1988). It belongs to a private collection and to my knowledge has never received any commentary other than a slightly overemphatic note in the catalogue of the sale.

22. Many thanks to Yolaine Escande, specialist in Chinese aesthetics and calligraphy, who was kind enough to look closely at this notebook and help me with her comments.

23. See with regard to this text Richard Sieburth's very reliable study "Signs in Action: The Ideograms of Ezra Pound and Henri Michaux" in this volume. An earlier version of this essay was published in Richard Sieburth, *Signs in Action Pound/Michaux*, New York (Red Dust) 1987, pp. 3–17.

24. By Jean-Dominique Rey, in *Henri Michaux. Œuvres choisies 1927–1984*, exhib. cat., Marseille, Musée Cantini, Réunion des Musées Nationaux, 1993, p. 213.

25. The text may be found in *Exorcismes*, Paris (Robert J. Godet) 1943, reissued in *Épreuves, exorcismes 1940–1944* in 1945 (*Œuvres complètes*, I, 1998, p. 885. The drawings, reissued in *Paintings and Drawings* with textual excerpts, are reproduced on pp. 930–33).

SIGNS IN ACTION: THE IDEOGRAMS OF EZRA POUND AND HENRI MICHAUX

Richard Sieburth

I WOULD LIKE TO BEGIN BY EVOKING A TRANSLATION that never saw the light. In his obituary memoir of Ezra Pound, Guy Davenport notes that during his final years in Venice *il miglior fabbro*, having abandoned his *Cantos* as a colossal botch, having edged further and further into silence, was nevertheless contemplating a translation of Henri Michaux's *Idéogrammes en Chine*. Pound's health was failing, as was his confidence in the word, and apparently after a few false starts the project was set aside. It was left to a younger American poet, Gustaf Sobin, to complete the task—with the result that Michaux's *Idéogrammes en Chine* was finally made available to English-speaking readers in 1984, published, appropriately enough, under the Poundian imprint of New Directions as a latterday complement (so the blurb reads) to Pound's and Ernest Fenollosa's classic study, *The Chinese Written Character as a Medium for Poetry*.[1]

Literary history is, of course, filled with such failed encounters—dialogues abandoned en route, aborted conversations—but it seems to me that the juncture of Pound and Michaux, however tenuous, however mute it might have been, is especially resonant, for here was Pound at the dusk of his career circling back to beginnings, returning once again to the ideograms he had first learned to haruspicate in 1913 with the aid of Fenollosa's manuscript on the Chinese character, and returning, moreover, in the company of a French poet whose own graphic and literary work had, since the late 1920s, been engaging the gist and gesture of Chinese ideogram with an intensity and an originality matched by few other artists of the twentieth century.

A translation of a French poet's meditations on Chinese calligraphy—the configuration is typically Poundian (think of the first Canto, a translation into Anglo-Saxonized English of a Renaissance Latin version of Homer). And if Michaux's French prose poetry acts as a mediator in this transaction between East and West, Chinese and English, this too is another memory of beginnings, a trace of the China Pound first discovered in French guise—whether it be via Pauthier's versions of Confucius or via Judith Gautier's *Livre de jade*, the delicate chinoiseries of which Pound would extend into the haiku-like condensations of the Imagist lyric or the poems of *Cathay* (1915). Pound's China, a realm where Mencius speaks to Mussolini and Confucius converses with the Adams dynasty in an idiom that blends the civic apothegms of the Encyclopedists with the hermetic evanescence of a Mallarmé, is an imaginary kingdom as quirky as any of those to be found in Michaux's *Voyage en Grande Garabagne*. I take Pound's late, silent dialogue with Michaux's *Idéogrammes en Chine* as a final, failed gesture toward this imaginary China—a last visit to the Empire of Signs (to use Barthes's term) or (if one prefers Genette) a belated *Voyage en Cratylie*.

Blanchot observes in an essay on Michaux and Borges that one of the tasks of criticism is to render all comparison impossible.[2] I would therefore like to proceed by simply juxtaposing, rather than explicitly comparing, Pound's and Michaux's encounters with the Chinese character, in the hope that such a juxtaposition might tell us something about larger issues involving modernism, Cratylism, and the poetics of the sign. I use the term juxtaposition deliberately because it is fundamental to what Pound calls the "ideogrammic method," a method that underlies both the formal and didactic design of the *Cantos*. Pound called his poetics "ideogrammic" because he followed the sinologist Fenollosa in believing (rightly or wrongly) that the sense of individual Chinese characters was visibly generated by the juxtaposition of their graphic (or graphemic) components. Fenollosa writes, for example:

> The ideograph "to speak" is a mouth with two words and a flame coming out of it. The sign meaning "to grow up with difficulty" is grass with a twisted root ... In this process of compounding, two things added together do not produce a third thing but suggest some fundamental relation between them. For example, the ideograph for a "messmate" is a man and a fire. [Fenollosa n.d., pp. 8–9]

The key term here is *relation*, for, as Fenollosa writes elsewhere in the same essay (predicting the structuralists): "Relations are more real and more important than the things they relate" (Fenollosa n.d., p. 22). Which Pound footnotes: "Compare Aristotle's Poetics: 'Swift perception of relations, hallmark of genius.'"

Such "swift perception of relations," associated by Aristotle with the intuition of metaphor, is what a poem like Pound's "In a Station of the Metro" of 1913 is out to record and instigate. The original printing emphasized the intervals that punctuate the poem, each semantic or rhythmic cluster functioning as a discrete, autonomous character, three characters to each line:

| The apparition | of these faces | in a crowd: |
| Petals | on a wet, black | bough. |

This technique of ideogrammic juxtaposition, still relatively simple and straightforward in Pound's "Metro" haiku, is applied at a number of levels in the *Cantos*. Only the scale of the units thus placed in relation changes, ranging from single works or tag phrases to complete lines or blocks of lines to entire Cantos or sequences of Cantos. Rather than explicitly articulating the syntactical (or narrative) connections between the items thus juxtaposed, rather than subordinating one to another (hypotaxis), Pound instead situates his material side by side on the same flat surface as equivalent units of design (parataxis). Pound's paratactic disposition of seemingly unrelated particulars has of course been frequently compared to modernist practices of collage or assemblage, but it is worth emphasizing that he conceived of his poetic method not only in the context of avant-garde experiment, but as a recovery of something profoundly traditional or archaic—after all, both the compound graphic and semantic structure of the Chinese character and the perfected parataxis of classical Chinese poetry seemed proof enough that other languages, other grammars of art were indeed possible.[3] Sergei Eisenstein, for one, came to similar conclusions about the unexplored linguistic possibilities of cinematic montage after studying Chinese ideograms, as witnessed by the title of his essay of 1929, "The Cinematographic Principle and Ideograph," a text roughly contemporary with Michaux's first graphic experiments with those imaginary alphabets or rebuses he would later term "ideogram compositions" or "cinematic drawings."[4]

Pound, Eisenstein, Michaux—a critical ideogram comprised of three names working in three different media, here assembled merely to indicate the extent to which the Chinese character, from the time of Leibniz all the way up to Sollers, has tended to speak primarily to Western *eyes* (and this despite the fact that 90% of Chinese characters are in fact *phonetic* compounds). The Imagist Pound was delighted to find in Chinese a language of signs so pictorially suggestive that his friend the French sculptor Gaudier-Brzeska could pick up a Chinese dictionary and effortlessly read the forms of many radicals at sight. Pound's mentor Fenollosa, steeped as he was in the American Transcendentalist tradition, encouraged his conviction that Chinese was a perfect natural language since it represented not sounds, but rather the "visible hieroglyphics" of Nature itself. Take, for example, Fenollosa's gloss on the Chinese sentence "Man sees horse."

> But Chinese notation is something much more than arbitrary symbols. It is based upon a vivid shorthand picture of the operations of nature. In the algebraic figure and in the spoken word there is no natural connection between thing and sign: all depends on sheer convention. But the Chinese method follows natural suggestion. First stands the man on his two legs. Second, his eye moves through space; a bold figure represented by running legs under an eye ... Third stands the horse on his four legs ... Legs belong to all three characters; they are alive. The group holds something of the quality of a continuous moving picture. [Fenollosa n.d., pp. 8–9]

人　見　馬

If one wanted to translate Fenollosa's analysis into Jakobsonian terms, one could say that according to this account, the poetic function of Chinese is foregrounded by the visual form of the signifier itself; one can actually *see* how the axis of selection (the legs the three characters have in common) has been projected onto the axis of combination. For Fenollosa the Chinese character is intrinsically poetic in another sense as well, for it bears "its metaphor on its face" (Fenollosa n.d., p. 25): the sign for sun glows like a sun, the sign for tree grows like a tree, and when you combine the two, entangling the sun radical in the branches of the tree, you have represented 'east.' One need only leaf through Genette's *Mimologiques* to recognize Fenollosa's mirage of a non-arbitrary, fully motivated language as a familiar avatar of Cratylism. Indeed, commenting on Claudel's "Religion du signe" of 1898 (included in *Connaissance de l'Est*) and his later *Idéogrammes occidentaux* (1926), Genette observes that the Chinese logogram has tended to play the same role in twentieth-century Cratylism that the Egyptian hieroglyph played in the nineteenth.[5]

Fenollosa's picture theory of Chinese, however, does not merely rest on the assumption of a one-to-one correspondence between the sign and what it represents; rather, he is more concerned with *groups* or *systems* of signs, with signs in relation, in movement, in process.[6] Hence the emphasis on Chinese as a cinematic "moving picture," on Chinese word order as a "transference of power" from agent to object, and hence the insistence that Chinese is composed not of nouns, but of verbs:

> A true noun, an isolated thing, does not exist in nature. Things are only the terminal points, or rather the meeting points, of actions, cross-sections cut through actions, snapshots. Neither can a pure verb, an abstract motion, be possible in nature. The eye sees noun and verb as one: things in motion, motion in things, and so the Chinese conception tends to represent them. [Fenollosa n.d., p. 10]

"Things in motion, motion in things"—the mimology proposed here is based less (to use Peirce's terminology) on the iconic resemblance between the sign and what it represents than on an indexical relation of causality or contiguity between the two. Indeed, if Fenollosa or Pound consider Chinese the ideal medium for poetry, it is because its characters actually mime or respond to the very processes of Nature in a language the signs of which are visibly patterned by the primal energies of the elements (much as, in Peirce's example of the indexical sign, the wind causes the weathervane to register its direction). Answering to a *natura naturans*, a nature in process, in the making, Chinese writing thus becomes a *scriptura scribens*, a writing in and of process. Fenollosa's post-Romantic insistence on *energeia* over *ergon* ("the verb must be the primary fact of nature," "The cherry tree is all that it does") not only had a great deal to do with Pound's own drift from aestheticism into activist politics (a poet is all that he does, however grievously he might err in the process), but it also served to shape his conception of the *Cantos* as a kind of gigantic action poem—not an autonomous textural artifact, not a noun, but a verb, an ongoing enactment of individual and collective process, a performative experiment open to whatever might at the moment be at hand, including its own incompletion or eventual ruin.

I have deliberately borrowed the notion of an action poem from the vocabulary of modern art history (it was Harold Rosenberg who was the first to speak of action painting)[7] because it provides an obvious bridge into Michaux—poet, painter, actor, in short, inscriber of actions or agons on canvas or page, performer of dramatic events that invite reading as signs, traces of movement, vestiges of gesture. Scholars of Michaux concur in emphasizing the centrality of *le geste* to his entire work—whether it be the onomatopoetic vocal gesticulations of Michaux's 'nonsense' verse or the calligraphic pantomime that is a trademark of his drawings.[8] Michaux describes as follows the process recorded in *Mouvements*, a series of some twelve hundred sheets of ideogrammic signs enacted in Indian ink over the course of 1950–51: "It involved gestures, interiors, for which we have no limbs at our disposal but only the desire of limbs, tensions, élans, all made up of living cords, never thick, never swollen with flesh or enclosed in skin."[9] Gestures incarnating, dramatizing something beyond or before the body, gestures realizing themselves in or as signs, the sheer generation or proliferation of which allows Michaux to leave words behind:

> On the contrary, it is through having freed me from words, those tenacious partners, that the drawings are frisky and almost joyous, that their movements came buoyantly to me even in exasperation. And so I see in them a new language, spurning the verbal, and so I see them as *liberators* … a writing unhoped for, affording relief, in which [one] will be able at last to express [one]self far from words, words, the words of others.[10]

To which one might juxtapose Julia Kristeva's essay on gesture in *Semiotike*, which addresses gestuality as an instance of sheer production, sheer expenditure, in other words, as a semiotic practice that puts into question not only the conventional communicative function of verbal language, but more crucially the phonocentric priority generally accorded to voice by Western linguistics and metaphysics.[11] Kristeva bases much of her notion of gesture on Tchang Tcheng-Ming's *L'Écriture chinoise et le geste humain* (1937), the very same book, it turns out, that inspired Claudel's "La Figure, le mouvement et le geste dans l'écriture en Chine et en Occident."[12] Although Kristeva wants to consider gesture not in terms of representation or expression, but rather as a kind of anaphora or index (in the Husserlian sense of *Anzeichen*), her vocabulary oddly echoes Fenollosa's: "Before and behind *voice* and *writing* there is anaphora: the gesture that *indicates*, that institutes *relations* and eliminates entities. The semiotic system of the Dogon [Kristeva's semiotopia now migrates from China to Africa], which in the end seems to be more a scriptural semantic system than a verbal one, is thus based on *indication*: for them, to learn to speak is to learn to indicate by tracing."[13]

This revisionary Derridean myth of origins, which stages the anteriority of *écriture* (writing, marking, tracing, drawing) to speech, brings us to Michaux's own *Fable des origines*, to quote the title of one of his earliest books (1923). In his semi-autobiographical *Émergences-Résurgences* (1972), he tells the origin story of his own career as a writer-painter. In the beginning was the line, the trace, the traversal and division of space:

> One day, late in life, I too feel the impulse to draw, to participate in the world by lines. One line, rather than many lines. And so I begin, allowing myself to be led by a single line, giving it free rein without so much as lifting pencil from paper—until, having wandered restlessly in this restricted space, it inevitably comes to a stop.[14]

This is line as sheer process, having no other motive than its own exploratory traversal of the field of the page. This nomadic, somnambulistic line, a kind of seismographic indicator of the aleatory psychic and physical vectors that have converged on the page, is Michaux's own version of Surrealistic automatic writing. But having given himself over to line, to pure *parcours* or *trajet*, Michaux soon finds himself confronting signs: pages emerge covered with imaginary alphabets (which he calls "pictographs" or "ideographs"), their squiggles and strokes arranged into furrows of writing.

Here is Michaux's retrospective account of these *Alphabets* or *Narrations* that he drew/wrote in 1927:

> Later, the signs, certain signs. Signs speak to me. I would gladly draw them, but a sign is also a stop sign. And at this juncture there is still something I desire above all else. A *continuum*. A murmur without end, like life itself, the thing that keeps us going ... I want my markings [*mes tracés*] to be the very phrasing [*le phrase*] of life, but supple, deformable, sinuous.[15]

On the one hand, Michaux's move from the single unbroken line into a series of signs embodies an attempt to discover a kind of language or semiotic system that goes beyond (or before) the conventionalized marks of writing or pictorial representation—a series of signifiers without signifieds (or rather, that would simply signify the desire to write, draw, inscribe, sign), a purely private alphabet that would free him from having to speak (to draw) like anybody else, a succession of signs that one might term *idio*grams (somewhat on the order of the neologistic idiolect he was experimenting with during this same period in the poems of *Qui je fus*). On the other hand, Michaux's discovery of signs is, as he notes, also an encounter with a certain kind of blockage or stoppage, for, as the continuous line breaks up into a sequence or grouping of signs, an impetus is lost, a fixity sets in, the flow of traffic now halted by stop signs—"*un signe, c'est aussi un signal d'arrêt.*"

Such stasis or arrest, of course, goes directly counter to Michaux's desire to embody a continuum, a *durée*, an unbroken murmur of motion—and the fact that he titles these imaginary alphabets or pictograms *Narrations* indicates just how far this aesthetic of continuity lies from Pound's paratactic ideograms, which aim instead at pulverizing the syntagms of narrative, at erasing transitions, at opening up intervals and breaches by a constructivist technique of collage or jumpcut montage that serves to isolate the signs thus juxtaposed. Michaux, by contrast, wants to surmount such segmentation, to eliminate the problematic space *in between* by the sheer rapidity of his traversal through it. His mescaline writings and drawings of the 1950s, for example, register a state of flux where there is virtually no intervening vacuum between images or marks, but rather a plenum of uninterrupted pulsations and oscillations.[16] Similarly, if Michaux's poetry favors prose lineation over lines of verse (and a prose, moreover, that is often narrative in thrust), it is largely because he is after a fluidity, a metonymic continuity or kinesis that will somehow enact the ongoing pulse or tempo of *l'élan vital*.

Michaux's early ideogrammic drawings, he tells us in *Émergences-Résurgences*, led to an impasse or *échec* that caused him to abandon painting altogether for a number of years. It was only in the course of his travel to the Far East in 1930–31 that he suddenly recognized what he had been looking for in his earlier explorations of lines and signs:

> But it is Chinese painting that enters into me in depth, converts me. As soon as I see it I become a complete adept of the world of signs and lines. Distances preferred to proximities, the poetry of incompletion preferred to eyewitness accounts, to copies. Markings launched into the air, fluttering as if caught by the motion of a sudden inspiration, and not prosaically, laboriously, exhaustively traced … this is what spoke to me, what seized me, what carried me away. This time, the cause of painting had been won.[17]

In *Un barbare en Asie*, Michaux's 1933 travelogue of this same journey, he similarly underscores the importance of this semiotic encounter with the exotic, for in China he discovered a tradition of painting, writing, and theater that was at once concrete and abstract, material and immaterial, stable and fluid—a tradition, in short, grounded not in mimesis, not in copying, but rather in the art of *signification*:

> The Chinese have a talent for reducing being to signified being (something like the talent for algebra or math). If a battle is to take place, they do not serve up a battle, they do not stimulate it. They signify it. This is the only thing that interests them, the actual battle would strike them as vulgar.[18]

Or, as Michaux later puts it in *Idéogrammes en Chine*: "No longer imitate nature. Signify it. By marks [*traits*], by élans." The French word *trait*, as Barthes observes, is a term shared both by the graphic arts and by linguistics.[19] It suggests a kind of diacritical marking that is fundamental to the Chinese conception of *wen*, a character that signifies a conglomeration of marks, whether these be the veins of stones or of wood, the strokes that connect stars into constellations, the tracks of animals on the ground, or finally, the art of writing, of literature, and of social courtesy.[20]

Michaux's 1931 visit to the Empire of Signs, according to his own account, verified his vocation as an adept of *wen*, as an adventurer in that semiotic no-man's-land that exists somewhere between (or perhaps before) visual and verbal language. An entire strand of Michaux's graphic work shows his drawing or painting constantly moving toward the territory of writing. His early *Alphabets* or *Narrations* of 1927 will resurface in the rebuses of *Épreuves, exorcismes 1940–1944* (1945), the ideogrammic élans of *Mouvements* (1951), the serial gouache bestiaries of 1952, the Indian and sepia ink canvases of 1961–62, the gouache calligrams of 1965–66, or the anthropomorphic acrylics and aquarelles of the 1970s. But if the graphic so often tends towards the graphemic in Michaux, the reverse is also true, perhaps nowhere more so than in the mescaline drawings of *Misérable miracle* (1956) in which the horizontal lettering of actual words on the page gradually disintegrates into a series of unintelligible vertical or transversal strokes that resemble the gibberish penmanship of a Saul Steinberg or the unreadable tags of a subway graffiti artist.

Michaux's explorations of the process whereby drawing or painting translate into writing and vice versa (to which one should also add his many books in which the illustrative relation of text to image is virtually reversible) prepare his return to China in *Idéogrammes en Chine* (1971), a late, mellow meditation on his own career in and among signs, an *ars poetica* that reads like an autumnal episode in the adventures of Monsieur Plume. *Idéogrammes en Chine* was initially written as an introduction to Léon Tchang Long-Yan's *La Calligraphie chinoise. Un art à quatre dimensions.*[21] The text therefore presents itself in the form of a commentary or, to quote the title of Michaux's book on Magritte, *En rêvant à partir de peintures énigmatiques* (1964), as a reverie inspired by the samples of Chinese calligraphy that intersperse his French text and provide the themes on which his commentary will play its variations. Just as Michaux takes Magritte's paintings and turns them into stories, so *Idéogrammes* links its visual pretexts into a chronicle evoking the genealogy and evolution of Chinese writing. Its overall plot may be summarized as follows: 1) writing at its origin, 2) the loss of origin, 3) the recovery of origin via etymology, 4) writing-as-representation moving toward writing-as-signification, and 5) the return, via abstraction, to Nature and origins. As this rough outline might make clear, Michaux's essay on the ideogram enacts a kind of dialectical oscillation between origin and derivation, absence and presence, representation and signification, a movement that leads in the end to an equilibrium or "just balance of opposites" embodied by calligraphy in its role as a "mediator" between "communication and suspension."

As in the Fenollosa–Pound essay on the Chinese character, a Cratylistic nostalgia haunts Michaux's meditations on calligraphy. After a brief introductory section that registers the inevitable bewilderment of the Western eye upon first encountering a page of Chinese calligraphy ("Lines going off in all directions. In every which way: commas, loops, curlicues, stress marks, seemingly at every point, at all levels: a bewildering thicket of accents"), Michaux passes beyond this stage of originary confusion to evoke the dawn of Chinese writing in the Chou Dynasty, the mythic era of *ku-wen* bronze inscriptions:[22]

> There was a time, however, when the signs still spoke, or nearly; when, already allusive, they revealed— rather than simple things or bodies or materials—groups, ensembles, situations.
> There was a time.

But this "primitive readability," this Golden Age of "the original reality, the concrete and its closely related signs," is succeeded by a period in which the "inclination toward concealing" and "the pleasure in abstraction" invade writing, as the stolid chisel of the bronze or stone engraver gives way to the nimble brush of the calligrapher: writing henceforth loses its open, public face to become an élite secret shared by the scribal initiate. Michaux's cadences grow noticeably elegiac:

> Withdrawal, self-absorption won out.
> Won out: the will to be mandarin.
> Gone, now, were those archaic characters that had stirred the heart. And those signs, so palpable, that had overwhelmed their own creators and amazed their very first readers.
> Gone, too, were the veneration and simplicity, the earliest poetry, the tenderness that arose from the surprise of the first 'encounter' …
> All contact cut, now, with the beginnings …
> Gone, now, were the 'heartfelt' characters, so dependent on reality. Vanished from usage, from language …

With the sign thus increasingly alienated from its natural model, the aura of the written character as ritual object or event now recedes: "Religion in writing was on the decline; the irreligion of writing had just begun." Sacred gives way to secular scripture.

But in this world of the Fall, where writing now functions as an agent of exclusion and concealment, there is nonetheless hope of redemption: as scholars piously regather the ancient characters into indexes (c. AD 120), a first etymological dictionary (the *Shuo-wen*) is born, restoring words to their origins, resurrecting the characters from their tombs of abstraction. At this etymological juncture, Michaux's text suddenly soars into a Whitmanesque (or Borgesian) catalogue of this rediscovered plenitude—an inventory of the wealth of a world again filled with people, things, events, signs:

> full of moons, and hearts, full of doors
> full of men who bow
> who withdraw, grow angry, and make amends
> full of obstacles
> full of right hands, of left hands
> of hands that clasp, that respond, that join forever
> full of hands facing hands
> of hands on guard, and others at work
> full of mornings
> full of doors

These anaphoras continue for two pages, a familiar variant on one of Michaux's favorite modes—the abecedarium, the bestiary, the taxonomy, the serial proliferation of signs. This profusion is made possible by an etymological perspective that resituates (or remotivates) the sign in relation to its source—as Fenollosa remarked, poets proceed by "feeling back along the ancient lines of advance," a process particularly evident in Michaux's own ideogrammic drawings and paintings, which are in a sense etymologies of gesture, enactments of their own origin, mimings of the moment at which signs, not yet fully bearers of sense, begin to *come into being*.

This explains, I think, why Michaux's allegorical history of the ideogram should now move from etymology into the next stage, the development of calligraphy—the sign in (or as) action. The increasingly stylized strokes of the calligrapher represent for Michaux a further (and higher) retreat from iconicity, from resemblance:

> For ages the Chinese had been subject, in this field and others, to the charm of resemblance: to an immediate resemblance, at first, and then to a distant one, and finally to the composition of resembling elements.
> An obstacle, as well: it had to be overcome.
> Even that the furthest resemblance. There was no returning; all similitude was to be abandoned forever.
> Another destiny awaited the Chinese.
> To abstract means to free oneself, to come disentangled.

Abstraction, associated earlier with secrecy and concealment and serving the hegemony of a scribal élite, now re-emerges as a religious ascesis or gnosis. Ritualized into the art of calligraphy, this action writing/painting completely dematerializes the world into a condition of pure speed, pure flight, pure mind: "The destiny that awaited Chinese writing was utter weightlessness." But if calligraphy enables the material body of the sign to be transfigured into pure spirit, the very activity of this *scriptura scribens* nonetheless plunges us back (by a kind of dialectical reversal) into the immanent energies of a *natura naturans*. Freed from imitating nature, signs may now signify it, respond to it, participate in its *wen*:

> No longer to imitate, but to signify nature. By strokes, darts, dashes.
> Ascesis of the immediate, of the lightning bolt.
> The sign in Chinese, today, which is no longer in any way mimetic, has the grace of its own impatience. It has drawn from nature its flight, its diversity, its inimitable way of knowing how to bend, rebound, redress itself.
> Like nature, the Chinese language does not draw any conclusions of its own, but lets itself be read …
> Characters open onto several directions at once.
> Point of pure equilibrium …
> Calligraphy in its role as mediator between communion and abeyance …
> Calligraphy around which—quite simply—one might abide as next to a tree, or a rock, or a source.

At the end of this long detour through China, Michaux thus rediscovers a modernist version of the ancient dream of Cratylus, a semiotopia in which all his works, all his gestures, all his *tracés* will bespeak *le phrasé* of natural process. The agons of his earlier work now give way to the late serenity of *Jours de silence* (1978), the sign pulsing at the heart of stillness:

> *Certitude vibrante*
> *sa touche si fine, qui fait signe*
> *cime et abîme sur la même ligne*
>
> Vibrant certainty
> its touch so fine, making a sign
> peak, abyss on the same line.

NOTES

This essay was delivered as a lecture at a colloquium on Michaux and Signs held at New York University in the spring of 1985. A slightly different version has been published in a special issue of *L'Esprit Créateur* devoted to the work of Henri Michaux.

   I would like to thank New Directions and Gustaf Sobin for permission to quote extensively from the English translation of Michaux's *Idéogrammes en Chine*.

1. *Idéogrammes en Chine* 1975; *Ideograms in China*, trans. Gustaf Sobin, New York (New Directions) 1984; Ernest Fenollosa, *The Chinese Written Character as a Medium for Poetry*, ed. Ezra Pound, San Francisco (City Lights) n.d. All subsequent page references to the Fenollosa will be included in the body of the text.
2. Maurice Blanchot, "L'Infini et l'infini," *Henri Michaux*, ed. Raymond Bellour, Paris (Éditions de l'Herne) 1966, p. 80.
3. For a fuller treatment of Pound's 'ideogrammic method' and its relation to the American tradition of Willimas, Olson, Duncan, Ginsberg, and Snyder, see Laszlo Géfin, *Ideogram: History of a Poetic Method*, Austin (University of Texas) 1982.
4. See Hugh Kenner, *The Pound Era*, Berkeley and Los Angeles, California, and London (University of California Press) 1971, p. 162.
5. Gérard Genette, *Mimologiques, Voyage en Cratylie*, Paris (Éditions du Seuil) 1976, p. 338.
6. It should be pointed out that the mimological mirage of the Chinese ideogram as a 'picture' of natural process is perhaps less crucial to Pound's actual handling of poetic language in his *Cantos* than it is to his economic theory, the major obsession of which turns on the issue of the accurate "monetary representation" or the faithful "money picture" of available goods. Not the least of the *Cantos*' many paradoxes lies in the fact that while the poem's central concerns involve the fate of the political or economic *representation* in the modern world, its actual linguistic texture is best described not in terms of *mimesis* but rather as *semiosis*, signs interpreting other signs. Michaux's meditations on the Chinese character are, as will be seen, informed by a similar oscillation between the notion of *representation* on the one hand, and that of *signification* on the other.
7. Harold Rosenberg, *The Tradition of the New*, New York (Horizon Press) 1959.
8. See, for example, Michel Beaujour, "Sens et nonsense" in the *Cahiers de l'Herne* devoted to Michaux, no.8, 1966, pp. 133–42, and Jean Starobinski, "Le Monde physionomique," *Henri Michaux*, Paris (Centre Georges Pompidou) 1974, pp. 65–67.
9. Pompidou 1974, p. 69. My translation.
10. Postface, *Mouvements* 1951.
11. Julia Kristeva, "Le Geste, pratique ou communciation?," *Semiotike*, Paris (Éditions du Seuil) 1969, pp. 29–51.

12. Jean-Claude Coquet, "La Lettre et les idéogrammes occidentaux," *Poétique*, no. 11, 1972, p. 401.

13. Kristeva 1969, p. 35.

14. *Émergences-Résurgence* 1972, p. 11. My translation.

15. *Ibid.*, p. 13.

16. See Malcolm Bowie, *Henri Michaux*, Oxford (Oxford University Press) 1973, pp. 161–63.

17. *Émergences-Résurgences* 1972, p. 16.

18. *Un barbare en Asie*, Paris (Gallimard) 1933, pp. 156–57. It might be noted in passing that this book was later translated into English by Sylvia Beach, friend of Pound and publisher of Joyce, New York (New Directions) 1949.

19. Roland Barthes, *L'Empire des signes*, Geneva (Éditions d'art Albert Skira) 1970, p. 7.

20. On *wen*, see Francoise Cheng, *L'Écriture poétique chinoise*, Paris (Éditions du Seuil) 1977, 9. 15, and Jacques Derrida, *De la grammatologie*, Paris (Éditions de Minuit) 1999 (1967), pp. 180–81.

21. Long-Yan 1971.

22. All the quotations from *Idéogrammes en Chine* are drawn from Gustaf Sobin's translation. Since the New Directions edition is unpaginated, page references have been omitted.

CHRONOLOGY

Leslie Jones

This chronology combines the complete text of Henri Michaux's "Some Information about Fifty-Nine Years of Existence" (shown in red ink), with additional biographical information culled from other sources. Citations for consulted texts are given below. Evident in a comparison of the two accounts is a number of discrepancies in dates and events, attributable most likely to Michaux's intended or unintended mis-remembrances. Unless otherwise noted, translations are by the author.

Sources: Henri Michaux, "Some Information about Fifty-Nine Years of Existence," Ball 1994; originally published as "Quelques renseignements sur cinquante-neuf années d'existence," in Robert Bréchon, *Michaux*, Paris (Collection La Bibliothèque Idéale, Gallimard) 1959. See also Maurice Imbert, "Repères biographiques," *Henri Michaux. Peindre, composer, écrire*, exhib. cat. by Jean-Michel Maulpoix and Florence de Lussy, Paris, Bibliothèque Nationale de France and Gallimard, 1999; Raymond Bellour and Ysé Tran, "Chronologie," *Magazine littéraire*, no. 364, April 1998, pp. 18–27; Brigitte Ouvry-Vial, *Henri Michaux, qui êtes-vous?*, Lyon (La Manufacture) 1989; René Bertelé, "Biography," trans. Elaine Harris, in Guggenheim/Pompidou 1978; and Geneviève Bonnefoi, "Biographie," *Henri Michaux. Peintre*, Ginals (Abbaye de Beaulieu) 1976.

1899

> May 24, 1899
> Namur (Belgium).
> Born into a middle-class family.
> Father from the Ardennes.
> Mother Walloon.[1]
> One of his grandparents, whom he never knew, of German origin.
> A brother, three years older.
> Distant Spanish ancestry.

Born Henri-Eugène-Marie-Ghislain Michaux to Jeanne-Marie-Constance Blanke (1869–1930) and Octave-Jean-Marie Michaux (1861–1930). His father was a merchant in Rochefort before his marriage and a hatter in Namur, although Michaux claims never to have seen his father work, describing him as "a man of independent means." Michaux has an elder brother, Marcel-Frédéric-Marie Michaux (1896–1945), who will become a lawyer in Brussels.

He is born with a weak heart, which he describes as having "holes in it," that will afflict him throughout his life.

1900–06
Brussels.
Indifference.
Inappetence.
Resistance.
Uninterested.

He avoids life, games, amusements, and variation.
Food disgusts him.
Odors, contacts.
His marrow does not make blood.
His blood isn't wild about oxygen.

Anemia.

Dreams, without images without words, motionless.
He dreams of permanence, of perpetuity without change.
His way of existing in the margins, always on strike, is frightening or exasperating.
He's sent to the country.

1906–10
Putte-Grascheide.
Little village in la Campine.[2]
Five years in boarding school.
Poor, tough, cold school.
Classes are in Flemish.
His classmates, sons and daughters of poor peasants.

Secretive.
Withdrawn.
Ashamed of what surrounds him, of everything that has surrounded him since he came into the world, ashamed of himself, of being only what he is, scorn for himself and for everything he has known up to now.
He is still disgusted by foods, wraps them in paper and stuffs them in his pocket. Once he's outside, he buries them.

1911–14
Brussels.
Returns to Brussels. Saved! So he does prefer one reality to another. Preferences begin.
Watch out! sooner or later, belonging to the world will come in. He is twelve.
Ant battles in the garden.
Discovery of the dictionary, of words that do not yet belong to phrases, to phrasemakers, masses of words, words he can use himself in his own way. Goes to a Jesuit school.

With his father's help, he becomes interested in Latin, a beautiful language, which sets him apart from others, transplants him: his first departure. Also the first sustained effort he enjoys.

Music, just a bit.

Attends Collège Saint-Michel, a Jesuit school. Among his classmates are the poet Norge, the playwright Herman Closson, and the writer Camille Goemans. According to Michaux, the Jesuits emphasize teaching of the humanities over the sciences, and what he learns about the art of Classical Greece and Rome, in particular, leaves him "indifferent," even "hostile," hating all that reproduces the "real." He is inspired rather by Chinese calligraphy and insects, which he would "examine at length under a magnifying glass from which he was never separated."[3]

1914–18
Brussels.
Five years of German occupation.
First French composition in school. A shock for him. The things he finds in his imagination! A shock even for the teacher, who pushes him toward literature. But he rejects the temptation to write; it could turn him away from the main point. What main point? The secret that, from his earliest childhood, he has suspected might exist somewhere. People around him are visibly unaware of it.

All kinds of reading. Research to discover his family, scattered through the world, his real parents, though not quite his parents either, to discover those who may "know" (Ernest Hello, Ruysbroek, Tolstoy, Dostoevsky).[4] Reads Lives of saints, the most surprising, the furthest removed from the average man. Also readings in bizarre writers, eccentrics or Jeune Belgique[5] who write in a strange style he would like to see still stranger. After his baccalaureate,[6] with the university closed because of the Occupation, two years of readings, of intellectual pottering about.

1919
First year of medical school.
Doesn't show up at the final exams. Gives up studying medicine.

When the university in Brussels reopens following the war, Michaux takes classes in physics, chemistry, and biology in preparation for the study of medicine. Unsatisfied with the mediocre level of education and the system of learning by heart, Michaux decides not to take the first-year final exams. This leads to an argument with his parents, who cut off financial support.

1920
Boulogne-sur-Mer.
Ships out as a sailor on a five-masted schooner.

Rotterdam.
Ships out a second time. On *Le Victorieux*, a ten-thousand-ton fine-looking vessel the Germans have just delivered to France.
There are fourteen of us in a little crew's cabin, in the bow. Amazing comradeship, unexpected, invigorating. Bremen, Savannah, Norfolk, Newport News, Rio de Janeiro, Buenos Aires.

On the way back from Rio, the crew complains about the food, refuses to go on and unanimously reports in sick. Out of solidarity, he leaves this lovely vessel ... thus missing the shipwreck that will take place twenty days later, south of New York.

Michaux's time spent as a merchant marine begins a lifetime fascination with the sea: "What I know, what is mine, is the indefinite sea."[7] Arriving in Rio, he falls from a ladder in the ship's hold and, after hospitalization, returns to Marseilles.

1921
Marseilles.
All over the world, ships (formerly used to transport troops and food) are being laid up. Impossible to find a job. The big window closes once again. He is obliged to turn away from the sea.
Back to the city and people he detests.
Disgust.
Despair. Various professions and jobs, all poor and poorly performed.
Top of his chart as a failure.

After global disarmament, Michaux is unemployed and, back in Brussels, takes a number of odd jobs, including school supervisor, editor, and taxi driver. In April he is inducted into the second regiment of grenadiers in Beverloo and enters officer reserve school in the fall. After six months he is declared unfit for service because of his heart condition.

1922
Brussels.
Reads (Lautréamont's) *Maldoror*.[8] Shock ... which soon brings on the long-forgotten need to write. First pages. Franz Hellens then Paulhan[9] see something in them, others see nothing at all.
Still reticent. He wouldn't like to 'have to' write.
It prevents dreaming. It makes him come out.
He prefers to remain coiled up.
Leaves Belgium for good.

1922–23   Publishes first text, "Cas de folie circulaire," in the Belgian literary journal *Le Disque vert* (September 1922). Part of this text is a myth describing the "Origin of Painting," republished in *Fables des origines* (1923). Over the next few years, Michaux contributes regularly to *Le Disque vert* and, in 1925, becomes the co-director in Paris. Other contributors include Blaise Cendrars, Jean Paulhan, André Malraux, Jean Cocteau, Vladimir Maïakowski, André Gide, Jules Supervielle, Francis Ponge, and Jacques Rivière. In 1923 publishes his first book, *Les Rêves et la jambe*, Anvers (Ça ira), and, at the end of the year, leaves Brussels for Paris.

1924
Paris.
He writes, but still ambivalent.

> Can't manage to find a pen name that would encompass him—him, his tendencies and his potentialities.
> He continues to sign with his ordinary name; he detests it, he is ashamed of it, like a label marked "inferior quality." Perhaps he hangs onto it out of faithfulness to his discontent and dissatisfaction. So he will never produce anything proudly, but always dragging that ball and chain at the end of each work, thus keeping him from even a slight feeling of triumph and achievement.

Meets Jules Supervielle and Jean Paulhan through Franz Hellens, and the three become lifelong friends. With Paulhan, in addition to writing, shares enthusiasm for Ping-Pong and the natural sciences. Paulhan becomes Michaux's contact in "*le monde parisien*" and a favorite reader and editor. Supervielle helps Michaux financially, hiring him occasionally as a secretary and as a tutor to his children, and inviting him regularly to his home (every Sunday for lunch) and to his vacation residences in Le Picquey and Port-Cros.

Meets André Breton while preparing the article "Notes sur le suicide, Énigmes, Surréalisme" for the January 1925 issue of *Le Disque vert*. Ambivalent about Surrealism's sensationalist strategies, Michaux shares their aim of challenging the status quo, stating, "the marvelous surrealist is monotonous but between the marvelous and whatever it is, I hesitate not. Long live the marvelous."[10]

1925

> Klee, then Max Ernst, Chirico … Extreme surprise. Up to now, he had hated painting and the fact itself of painting, "as if there still weren't enough of reality, of that awful reality," he used to think. "But to want to repeat it, to come back to it!"
> Various jobs. In a publishing house for a while, production department.

Max Ernst and Paul Klee got me interested in painting about the same time, when I was twenty-four. Until then I had strongly rejected it. I hated painters more than anyone else as I considered them as being the voluntary helpers of cumbersome reality and its appearances, which form an all-too-conspicuous screen (even the cubists had never got beyond them, on the contrary). At last, thanks to Ernst and Klee, I was able to get a glimpse of what goes on behind the scenes. It was a way, a hope. So it was possible to do something with Western painting, which had been "employed" until then.[11]

Makes first attempts at painting in a variety of media.

About this time meets Brassaï and the writer and photographer Claude Cahun, who teaches him English. Cahun is the first of but a few photographers he agrees to sit for. Becomes interested in Annamese (Vietnamese).

1927

> Quito.
> Year's trip to Ecuador, with Gangotena, an Ecuadorian poet possessed by genius and ill luck. He dies young and after him his poems, most of them unpublished, burnt up in a plane crash, disappear forever.

Publishes his first important book, *Qui je fus*, Paris (Collection Une Œuvre, un Portrait, Gallimard), a compilation of texts previously published in journals such as *La Revue européenne, Les Cahiers du Sud, Commerce,* and *La Nouvelle Revue française* between 1924 and 1927.

A line drawing—the first to be reproduced—is published in "Hommage à Léon-Paul Fargue," included in the June issue of *Les Feuilles libres.* Another drawing is reproduced a few months later in conjunction with his text "Ensoufflement" in the August–September issue of *Les Cahiers du Sud.*

First 'signs' drawings, *Alphabet* and *Narration,* are compositions of vaguely pictorial signs that resemble writing, yet are indecipherable. Such 'writings' reflect his interest in notions of universal language and anticipate his later use of signs in the Alphabets (*c.* 1943) and Mouvements (1950) series. After these initial attempts, Michaux virtually abandons painting and drawing until 1934.

> I get something from signs. I would gladly draw some, but a sign is also a stop signal ... I draw instead what resemble pictograms, or rather pictographic coursings, but without rules. I want my tracings to be the very phasing of life, but flexible, but deformable, sinuous ... On seeing them, those around me, well-wishers, shook their heads in embarrassment ... I was on the wrong track ... instead of writing and leaving it at that.
>
> What corresponded to an extreme need that seemed to me as natural as the need for bread, water, and sleep, did not correspond to any need for bread, water, and sleep, did not correspond to any need in those around me. They did not see much besides the awkwardness and the timidity of my renderings.
>
> How could it be otherwise? How could I dare to brave the paper just like that?
>
> What an impertinence to want to!
>
> Drawing had no part in my upbringing. These are my first sallies. I have to get used to the steerer's impudence. Misses. Not entirely (a certain embryo ... perhaps for later on). I give up. I put my desire to sleep. I go on a few voyages. The source of writing has not run dry, calls itself back to me.[12]

Departs Amsterdam on December 28 for Guayaquil, Ecuador via Panama aboard the *Boskoop* with Alfredo Gangotena, an Ecuadorian poet and close friend that Michaux met in 1927.

1928
    Paris.

Arrives in Quito, Ecuador on January 28. Throughout his year-long stay in South America, sends texts recounting his experiences to Jean Paulhan that will eventually be published as *Ecuador,* Paris (Gallimard) 1929. Suffers physically in the mountain climate but continues strenuous travels nonetheless.

> I believed, perhaps confusedly, in justifying my existence by navigating the long course [of the river] or traveling the Napo (a tributary of the Amazon) in a dugout canoe, by scaling mountains and volcanoes in the Andean cordillera. I ill-treated myself. I made myself walk, but my body responded badly to the adventures.[13]

Begins reading the works of the Tibetan Buddhist master Milarépa (1040–1123). The writings of this "*fameux bonhomme*" ("famous fellow")[14] become his "bedside reading."[15]

1929
    His father dies. Ten days later, his mother dies. Voyages to Turkey, Italy, North Africa ...
    He travels *against*.

> To drive his country out of him, his attachments of all kinds and whatever elements of
> Greek or Roman culture or Belgian habits have become attached to him, despite himself.
> Voyages of expatriation.
> Still, his rejection begins to yield just a bit to the desire for assimilation.
> He will have a lot to learn, to learn to open up. It will take a long time.

1929–30 *Mes propriétés* published by Jacques-Olivier Fourcade, who would become a lifelong friend. Over the years Michaux will frequently work and reside in the studio-converted garage adjacent to the Fourcade residence in Meudon.

Death of Michaux's father in Forest, Belgium, on March 10, 1930. His mother dies later that same month on March 29 in Uccle, Belgium. Michaux sells his half of the family home to his brother and uses the money to travel. While abroad he invents the character Plume—the protagonist of *Un certain Plume*, Paris (Éditions du Carrefour) 1930.

> 1930–31
> in Asia.
> At last his voyage.
> India, the first people who, massively, seem to correspond to what is essential, at last a
> people that deserve to be distinguished from the others.
> Indonesia, China, countries about which he writes too quickly, out of his excitement and
> amazement at having been so deeply touched, countries about which he will then have to
> think and ruminate for years.

1931–33 Departs for an eight-month tour of Asia on November 9. His impressions of India, Nepal, Ceylon (Sri Lanka), China, Japan, Malaysia, and Indonesia are recounted in *Un barbare en Asie*, Paris (Gallimard) 1933. During this trip Michaux will develop a lifelong interest in Asian art, culture, and philosophy. Learns breathing exercises and how to meditate in Chandernagor, India, and in China "takes pleasure" in Tao and the readings of Lao-Tzeu.[16] His experiences in India and China so move him that he once claims he would not be bothered in the slightest if Europe were one day "swallowed up."[17]

Upon his return to Paris in the fall of 1932 he immerses himself in Hindu and Chinese texts and refuses an invitation to visit Paulhan and Supervielle in Port-Cros, stating, "I must go to work at the Musée Guimet."[18]

> 1932
> Lisbon–Paris

1934 Publishes "Dessins commentés" in *La Nouvelle Revue française* (*NRF*). Michaux's first text, based on ten of his own drawings, is republished in *La Nuit remue*, Paris (Gallimard) 1935, and announces Michaux's return to making art after seven years. Travels in Spain and meets Salvador Dalí and André Masson in Barcelona. Arrives in Lisbon in October and stays for an extended four months. He describes Portugal as the first country where nothing "wounds" him.[19] He spends most of his time writing and making drawings that will eventually appear in

Entre centre et absence (Henri Matarasso) 1936.

1935
  Montevideo, Buenos Aires.

Becomes a member of the editorial board of *Mesures* while continuing to contribute to *Les Cahiers du Sud* and the *NRF*. Publishes *La Nuit remue*, which receives wide critical attention (with reviews by Pierre Leyris, Michel Leiris, René Daumal, and Maurice Saillet) and establishes Michaux as a known writer.

Meets Doctor Gaston Ferdière, a psychiatrist, and his wife Marie-Louise (née Termet) at the home of Claude Cahun and Suzanne Malherbe. Attends Ferdière's *"présentations de malades"* at Sainte-Anne, where the doctor is working with Lacan. Marie-Louise is impassioned by music and art. She is a student of art historian Henri Focillon and takes courses at l'Institut d'Art et d'Archéologie at the Ecole du Louvre. Termet and Michaux will eventually marry in 1943.

1936   Since January 1 I have been working with gouache. Yes, this January 1 was the day of my Eureka. I found my way of painting (it's to use brush and water)! and we will see ... what we will see!![20]

Becomes a member of the editorial board of *Hermès*, a Belgian review devoted to poetry, philosophy, and mysticism. From 1937 to 1939 he will act as the editor-in-chief.

Refused the Prix Albert 1er on the pretext that the poem "Mon roi" in *La Nuit remue* is perceived by one of the members of the jury as an insult to the Belgian king.

First sojourn in Colpach, Luxembourg, at the home of Aline Mayrisch Saint-Hubert, woman of letters and wife of a Luxembourg industrialist. She and Michaux share interests in Asia, Zen philosophy, poetry, and mystics such as the fourteenth-century German Maître Eckart. Michaux sojourns regularly at her chateau in Colpach until her death in 1947. On the tenth anniversary of her death Michaux writes in homage: "Of her, more than of anyone, I am happy to say that 'we had been friends.'"[21]

Publishes *Entre centre et absence* (Henri Matarasso), the first book to include reproductions of his drawings (eight, including a frontispiece).

Departs for Argentina in July with Supervielle to attend the XIVth Congress of PEN CLUBS of Buenos Aires, where he delivers a lecture titled "L'Avenir de la poésie."

Meets Jorge Luis Borges in Buenos Aires. Borges will translate *Un barbare en Asie* for Éditions SUR (1941).

Travels to Uruguay where he meets Susana Soca, a poet and translator, and the only daughter of a wealthy and renowned Uruguayan doctor. Michaux would like to marry her but doesn't want to move to South America. For a short while he becomes the lover of Angelica Ocampo, the younger sister of Victoria Ocampo, director of the Argentinian literary review *SUR*.

1937
  Begins to draw more than from time to time. First show. (Galerie Pierre in Paris.)

Begins series of paintings executed in brightly colored gouache or pastel on black backgrounds (1937–39), depicting mysterious landscapes and figures. Sixteen of these paintings will be reproduced in *Peintures* (GLM, 1939), along with seven poems. "Black is his crystal ball," wrote Michaux, "from black alone can he see life emerge. A completely imaginary life."[22]

Marie-Louise attempts suicide after she and Michaux discuss breaking off their liaison. Michaux arrives in time to call firemen and save her.

First exhibition of paintings and drawings at the Librairie-Galerie de la Pléiade, Paris.

> My exhibition had a certain success, but few sales. These gentlemen want first to convince themselves that it's not simply an infatuation on my part. I'm preparing another nightmare exhibition for them in October.[23]

1938 Exhibition of gouache paintings at Galerie Pierre, Paris. The announcement card reads: "A POET CHANGES INTO A PAINTER."[24]

1938–39
 Meudon.
 Edits the review *Hermès*.

1939
 Brazil (Minas Geraes and the State of Rio).

Publishes *Peintures* (GLM), which includes seven poems and reproductions of sixteen paintings (black backgrounds and watercolors).

> The transfer of creative activities is one of the strangest of all voyages into the self ... . You change clearing stations when you start painting.
> The word-factory (thought-words, picture-words, emotion-words, motor-words) disappears, is simply, dizzyingly drowned. It no longer exists.[25]

Departs for Brazil in July where he stays six months. He is joined by Marie-Louise Ferdière in October. Writes *Au pays de la magie*, Paris (Gallimard) 1941, and makes drawings, nineteen of which will appear in *Arbre des tropiques*, Paris (Gallimard) 1942.

January 1940
 Back to Paris. In July, the exodus (of refugees from the Germans).
 Saint Antonin. Then Le Lavandou.[26]

1940 Works in the garage-atelier of the Fourcade residence in Meudon.

> I am writing from my garage, reduced at this moment to its simplest state, without heat, without light other than that of two candles, with rheumatism of the fingers, but not without spiders.[27]

On June 3 bombs fall very close to the Fourcade home, and on June 7 Michaux departs as a refugee for the South of France. He spends a few months in Saint-Antonin before moving into the residence assigned to him by the Vichy government in Le Lavandou (Villa Ar-mor). This will remain his official residence until July 1943. During this time he will travel only to

Marseilles and Cabris, near Grasse, where Mme. Mayrisch with André Gide and others have sought refuge.

1941–42
  Le Lavandou with the woman who will soon be his wife.

A lecture by André Gide on Michaux's character Plume is to be delivered in Nice on June 21, 1941, but is canceled by the Légion des Combattants, "not because this Plume is perfectly unknown, but because of his (Gide's) personal morality."[28] The written version is published shortly thereafter as *Découvrons Henri Michaux*, Paris (Gallimard) 1941.

Paints a series of watercolors (*c.* 1941–43) depicting expansive landscapes (some with figures) and begins a series of "the most nightmarish heads that you've ever seen."[29] Because Michaux, as a Belgian citizen, is unable to obtain permission to travel, Marie-Louise brings recent paintings to Paris for the exhibition of June 1942 at the Galerie de l'Abbaye (Galerie Zack). During the opening a group of students from the École des Beaux-Arts, accompanied by their professor, M. Poughéon, cause a scandal. One of the students shouts repeatedly, "This is disgusting. This is shit."[30] When asked to leave by Maurice Saillet, the student refuses, a fight breaks out, and the police are called to intervene. Upon hearing of the scandal, Michaux wrote to Saillet: "Well done! One can't always help oneself from beating up these Beaux-Arts types. Reactionaries are the Perpetual Enemy. But to want to obtain more from them is useless. Even in death they undoubtedly take the wrong direction."[31]

Divorce of Marie-Louise from Gaston Ferdière (on July 12).

1943
  Back to Paris. German Occupation (the second one).

Grows increasingly restless sequestered in Le Lavandou, where there are "few lectures. Few people of knowledge ..." and he experiences more and more "fits of rage."[32]

On July 3, after a long negotiation, Michaux finally receives permission to return to Paris.

Visits Picasso in his studio with Brassaï, and asks Paulhan to take him to the studios of Jean Fautrier and Georges Braque.

Marries Marie-Louise on November 15, with Paulhan and Marianne Rusen as witnesses.

Publishes *Exorcismes* (Robert J. Godet), with reproductions of eleven drawings. Among the drawings are new attempts at ideograms or "alphabets."

1944
  His brother dies.

Begins series of *frottages* created by randomly rubbing lead on paper, often over/against a textured surface. "Draw without anything particular in mind, scribble mechanically," Michaux declared, "almost always, faces will appear on the paper."[33] In this series executed between 1944 and 1947, bizarre anthropoid images emerge through this automatic drawing process, discovered by the Surrealist Max Ernst—an artist Michaux had admired since the 1920s. Seven of Michaux's *frottages* will be reproduced in *Apparitions* ("Le Calligraphe," Collection Le Point du Jour, Gallimard) 1946.

Publishes *Le Lobe des monstres*, Lyon (L'Arbalète), with a line drawing titled *Plume* as the frontispiece, and *Labyrinthes* (Robert J. Godet), with reproductions of fourteen line drawings.

Exhibition at Galerie Rive Gauche, Paris.

1945

Weakened by food shortages, his wife catches tuberculosis. Together in Cambo. Improvement.

Begins series of pen and ink drawings on watercolor wash. Exploiting the fluidity of the watercolor medium, Michaux's line bleeds, loosely defining forms in seeming metamorphosis from insect to human, human to insect. Examples of these drawings will be reproduced the following year in *Peinture et dessins*. Michaux continues making drawings in this manner over the next five years, with a notable increase in production following the death of his wife in 1948.

Death of his brother in Brussels on May 30.

Publishes "Combat contre l'espace" in the French literary and art review *Vrille*—his first text since "Origine de la peinture" (1922) to be devoted to the topic of painting—and *Épreuves, exorcismes 1940–1944*, Paris (Gallimard), which unites three collections published during the war: *Exorcismes*, *Labyrinthes*, and *Le Lobe des monstres*.

1946 Marie-Louise contracts tuberculosis, and she and Michaux spend several months in Cambo in the Pyrenees.

Publishes *Apparitions*, which contains reproductions of seven *frottages*. It is the first book conceived with René Bertelé, who will become an important editor and organizer of many of Michaux's exhibitions.

Exhibition of drawings at Galerie Rive Gauche, Paris.

Seghers publishes Bertelé's *Henri Michaux*. This book will serve as the single most important reference work on Michaux until Robert Bréchon's 1959 book.

Publishes *Peintures et dessins* (Collection Le Point du Jour, Gallimard), with reproductions of forty-four works combined with extracts from poems and an important preface—"En pensant au phénomène de la peinture"—that outlines Michaux's ideas on art, including "FANTOMISME."

> If I liked Isms and became captain of some individuals, I would surely launch a school of painting, PHANTOMISM (or 'psychologism').
> The face has traits. I don't give a damn. I paint the traits of the double (who doesn't necessarily need nostrils and can have a framework of eyes).
> I also paint the colors of the double, it's not necessarily on the cheeks or lips that he has red, but in a place where is his fire …

... what I would like is to paint the color of the temperament of others. That is to make the portraits of temperaments.[34]

The original gouaches and watercolors reproduced in *Peintures et dessins* are exhibited at Librairie-Galerie La Hune, Paris.

Contributes a watercolor and three *frottages* from *Apparitions* to an auction organized to raise funds for Antonin Artaud's living expenses.

Jean Dubuffet paints several portraits of Michaux.

1947
Almost cured. Voyages of convalescence and forgetting about troubles, in Egypt.

Exhibition at Guilde du Livre, Basel.

1948 Marie-Louise's nylon robe catches fire when it comes in contact with an electric heater and she is severely burned.

> An accident. Serious. Very serious. Involving someone close to me. Everything comes to a halt. Reality does not make much sense anymore, the other reality, that of diversion, which has no truck with Death. In a hospital fate stands still. No change for better or worse. My days are spent there. I try not to see, not to let it be seen that Death ... but that word will never be pronounced. I must instill hope, courage. Returning one evening from the hospital, weak and exhausted after spending the day there, I think of looking at some pictures. At least I think that's what I'm going to do. I open a portfolio. It contains a few reproductions of works of art. To hell with them! I sling them away. I can no longer get into them. A few sheets of white paper come next. Changed as well. Immaculate, they seem foolish, hateful, pretentious to me, unrelated to reality. In a black mood I start, having grabbed one, to cover it with a few dark colours and sullenly to squirt water onto it at random, not in order to do anything in particular, and certainly not a painting. I have nothing to do, I have only to undo. To undo the world of confused, conflicting things in which I am plunged.[35]

February 1948
Death of his wife as a result of atrocious burns.

Following his wife's death, executes hundreds of ink drawings on watercolor wash at an incredibly rapid speed, described by the writer and art collector Henri-Pierre Roché: "His inspiration came so fast that sometimes he threw aside with his left hand the painting he had just finished and simultaneously started another with his right hand."[36]

One hundred and sixty-five ink and wash drawings are exhibited at the Galerie René Drouin, Paris. The exhibition brings increased recognition of his art.

Begins experimenting with lithography, and in the fall publishes *Meidosems* (Collection Le Point du Jour, Gallimard), illustrated with reproductions of thirteen lithographs (including the cover).

1949 Further explores the expressive potential of watercolor, mostly in red and black. Exhibits recent watercolors at the Galerie René Drouin, Paris.

Publishes *Poésie pour pouvoir* (René Drouin) which contains a frontispiece by Michaux and linogravures by Michel Tapié.

Un barbare en Asie published in English as *A Barbarian in Asia*, trans. Sylvia Beach (New Directions).

1950 Returns to exploration of 'signs' that began in 1927 with a series of approximately twelve hundred pages covered with ink markings, sixty-four of which will be published in *Mouvements* (1951).

> They were gestures, interior gestures, the ones with which we don't have limbs but desires for limbs, stretching, impulsive movements and all this with living ligaments that are never thick, never big with flesh nor enclosed in skin ... What an experience it will be when the time is ripe at last and, having got into the habit of thinking in signs, we are able to exchange secrets with a few natural strokes like a handful of twigs.[37]

Publishes *Lecture par Henri Michaux de huit lithographies de Zao Wou-Ki* (Euros et Robert J. Godet), his first series of poems based on the work of another artist. Publishes *Passages*, an anthology of previously published writings, focused primarily on art. A revised and expanded version will appear in 1963.

1951–1952–1953
   He writes less and less, he paints more.

1951 First retrospective exhibition, *Pour mieux connaître Henri Michaux (1937–1951)*, at Galerie Rive Gauche, Paris.

The Space Within published in English (New Directions; trans. Richard Ellmann).

Publishes *Mouvements* (Collection Le Point du Jour, Gallimard), which includes a poem, preface, and reproductions of sixty-four pen and ink drawings.

> I'm not too sure what they are, these signs that I've produced. I am perhaps the least fit to speak of them, close to them as I am. I had covered twelve hundred pages with them and was aware only of their surge and flow when René Bertelé got hold of them and, cautiously, reflectively, discovered that they seemed to form sequences ... and so this book came about, more his work than mine.
>
> But what of the signs? It was like this: I had been urged to go back to composing ideograms, which I had been doing on and off for twenty years and the pursuit of which seems indeed to be part of my destiny, but only as a lure and fascination. Over and over again I had abandoned them for lack of any success.
>
> I tried once more, but gradually the forms 'in movement' supplanted the constructed forms, the consciously composed characters. Why? I enjoyed doing them more. Their movement became my movement. The more there were of them, the more I existed. The more of them I wanted. Creating them, I became quite other. I invaded my body (my centers of action and repose). It's often a bit remote from my head, my body. I held it now, tingling, electric. Like a rider on a galloping horse that together make but one ...[38]

1952 Executes a group of gouache paintings composed of numerous expressive black marks resembling stick figures, similar to many of the 'signs' in the *Mouvements* series. Piled together, these essentially abstract configurations have often been described as scenes of "crowds" ("*foules*") or "battles" ("*batailles*").

1953 Begins a series of 'signs' executed in gouache, which are exhibited at Galerie Nina Dausset, Paris.

1954 Makes first 'blot' paintings in ink. "One day I finally did it straight out. I emptied it out of the bottle with jerky movements and let it spread."[39] The blot paintings and subsequent large-format ink drawings would lead many to associate Michaux with the French movement known as "Tachisme." The artist rejected such an affiliation, stating: "If I'm a 'tachiste,' I'm one who can't stand '*taches*.'"[40] For Michaux, the blot functioned as a means, not an end. "I busy myself with curing the blots. The blots are a provocation. I meet it. Quickly. One must act quickly with those big limp ones that are apt to go wallowing everywhere. The crucial minute comes quickly. Quickly, before they extend their realm of abjectness and vomiting. Unbearable blots."[41]

Exhibition of ink paintings at Galerie René Drouin, Paris. First US exhibition at the Dussane Gallery, Seattle.

Naturalized French on August 27.

Publishes "Aventures de lignes," preface to Will Grohman's *Paul Klee*, Geneva (Coédition Flinker/Trois Collines).

First experience with the drug mescaline, an alkaloid from the mescal cactus plant found in Mexico. Over the next few years he will produce numerous drawings, paintings, and writings in an attempt to render the experience of his altered state. The drawings are most frequently executed in a thin, agitated line, like that of a seismograph, which seems to track interior pulsations and vibrations. The paintings in oil are fewer in number and are an attempt to render the experience as the effect of the drug fades away. Written accounts of his drug use, often including reproductions of mescaline drawings, are published in several books: *Misérable miracle* (1956), *L'Infini turbulent* (1957), *Paix dans les brisements* (1959), *Connaissance par les gouffres* (1961), *Les Grandes Épreuves de l'esprit* (1966). He will also experiment with hashish, LSD, ritaline, and psilocybin.

Mescaline made me realize that I was too often contented with little.[42]

Mescaline multiplies, sharpens, accelerates, intensifies the inward moments of becoming conscious.[43]

1955
Naturalized French.

1956
First experiment with mescaline.

Publishes *Misérable miracle*, Monaco (Éditions du Rocher), which includes reproductions of forty-eight mescaline drawings. An exhibition of mescaline drawings, titled *Description d'un trouble*, takes place at the Librairie-Galerie La Hune, Paris.

Travels to Egypt and Sudan on the occasion of an exhibition of watercolors at the Maison de la Culture Française in Cairo.

The exhibition *Parcours: Henri Michaux, 1939 à 1956* is held at Galerie René Drouin, Paris. Exhibitions also held at the Ruth Moskin Gallery, New York, and Galleria d'Arte Selecta, Rome.

Publishes *Quatre cents hommes en croix*, Sainte-Maurice-d'Ételan (Pierre Bettencourt), with reproductions of three drawings (including a frontispiece).

1957
Art shows in the United States, Rome, London.
Breaks right elbow. Osteoporosis. Hand unusable. Discovery of 'left man.'[44] Cured. And now?
Despite so many efforts in so many directions all through his life to change himself, his bones, without paying any attention to him, blindly follow their familial, racial, Nordic evolution …

Exhibition at Studio Paul Facchetti with Dubuffet and Wols. Exhibitions also held at the Galerie René Drouin, Paris (with Bettencourt and Dubuffet), the Palais des Beaux Arts, Brussels, and Gallery One, London.

Publishes *L'Infini turbulent* (Mercure de France), with reproductions of eleven mescaline drawings.

Publishes "The Thin Man," a poem about "looking at engravings by Matta," in the Italian journal *Botteghe oscure*.[45]

Michaux's work appears on cover of the journal *Quadrum*, no. 3, which also includes his essay "Vitesse et Tempo" on drawing, with reproductions of ink and mescaline drawings.[49]

The composer Pierre Boulez proposes a musical project conceived from Michaux's *Poésie pour pouvoir* (1949). He would like "to scalp language through [the use of] 'revealing' methods (electro-acoustical)."[46] The piece will be performed in Germany on October 19, 1958.

Michaux breaks his right arm in Valberg. "Right hand still paralyzed. Complications with arm, knees. Walking nearly impossible. Arthritis, *etc.* Total insomnia. NO WORK POSSIBLE."[47] From this experience he discovers his "left-side man" ("*homme gauche*") and writes "Bras cassé."[48]

Mescaline drawings become more figurative.

1958 Begins series of large ink paintings that seem to combine elements from earlier ink paintings, namely blots and "signs," in predominately horizontal formats.

Exhibition at Galleria dell'Ariete, Milan.

1959 Susana Soca dies in a plane accident.

Publishes *Vigies sur cible* (Éditions du Dragon), with nine etchings by Matta, and *Paix dans les brisements* (Flinker), with reproductions of twelve mescaline drawings.

Publication of Robert Bréchon's *Henri Michaux*.

First exhibitions at Galerie Daniel Cordier in Paris and Frankfurt. Exhibition includes mescaline drawings, gouaches, and watercolors, but it is the new large ink works begun the preceding year that attract the most attention. Cordier will exhibit Michaux's works almost every year until 1965. Exhibitions also held at Galerie Charles Lienhard, Zürich, and Galerie André Droulez, Reims.

> I am asked why I choose painting as a means ... First, I chose it in order to be encumbered ... also the will to enter into a domain behind which I slam the door of literature ... In painting I don't feel overcome. Nonetheless, the large black ink paintings are also confessions, but confessions of the moment, of a single moment ...[50]

1960 Exhibits at the Venice Biennale and receives the Einaudi Prize.

Contributes poem "Sous les yeux" as preface to *Joseph Sima* exhibition catalogue (Galerie Paul Facchetti).

Exhibitions at Galerie Blanche, Stockholm, and Galleria Blu, Milan.

1961 Continues making 'signs' by experimenting with different supports, like canvas and Japanese paper, and materials, like sepia and gouache. Also begins to lay down ink washes indicating horizontal rows or registers on which he lines up numerous 'signs.'

Contributes large ink drawing to auction organized to benefit Georges Bataille.

Publishes *Connaissance par les gouffres* (Collection Le Point du Jour, Gallimard).

Meets Micheline Phankim, who will become his companion and executor.

1962 Publishes *Vents et poussières* (Karl Flinker), with reproductions of nine mescaline drawings.

Retrospective held at the Silkeborg Museum in Denmark. Exhibitions also held at Galerie Daniel Cordier, Paris, and Galleria Notizie, Turin.

1963 Makes film, *Images du monde visionnaire*, with Eric Duvivier on his experiences with mescaline and hashish. Produced by Sandoz Laboratories.

First voyages with Micheline Phankim: Morocco (February, July–August, November), India and Nepal (December–January 1964). They will then travel each winter on a grand voyage (Asia, Africa, America) and each spring to a Mediterranean country.

Misérable miracle is translated into English by Louise Varèse and published by City Lights, publishers of the Beat poets.

Numerous exhibitions held worldwide: Robert Fraser Gallery, London; Cordier-Ekstrom Gallery, New York; Libreria Einaudi, Rome; Galerie de Buren, Stockholm; and Galerie Van de Loo, Munich.

1964 *Henri Michaux ou l'espace du dedans*, a film about Michaux's art, is made by Geneviève Bonnefoi and Jacques Veinat. The film is shown as part of Michaux's 1966 exhibition at the Galerie Engelberts in Geneva.

First major retrospective at the Stedelijk Museum, Amsterdam. Another retrospective is held at Galerie Motte, Geneva.

Publishes "En rêvant à partir de peintures énigmatiques," an ensemble of texts conceived from paintings by Magritte, in the journal *Mercure de France*.[51] Republished as *En rêvant à partir de peintures énigmatiques*, Montpellier (Fata Morgana) 1972.

1965 Major retrospective of more than two hundred and fifty paintings and drawings at the Musée d'art moderne de la ville de Paris. Exhibitions also held at Gimpel Hanover, Zürich, and Cordier-Ekstrom Gallery, New York.

Becomes a member of Dubuffet's "Compagnie de l'art brut."

Michaux refuses the Grand Prix national des lettres.

1966 Returns to drawing in the style of the mescaline drawings, without actually being under the influence of the drug. (He does so again in 1969.) "Those who have once experienced the visions and the fascinating passivity cannot forget. Mescaline is not, however, indispensable. Without it I have several times been able to have visions. The brain is able, and must be able, to reproduce everything that it has experienced."[52] To differentiate them from the earlier works, he first calls them "disaggregation" ("*désagrégation*") drawings, later modifying the term to "reaggregation" ("*réagrégation*") drawings.

Exhibition at the Galerie Le Point Cardinal with Artaud and Ernst. First exhibition of disaggregation drawings. This exhibition marks the beginning of a long collaboration with Jean Hugues who will exhibit Michaux's work regularly at Le Point Cardinal. Exhibitions also held at Galerie Edwin Engelberts, Geneva, and Galerie Rudolf Zwirner, Cologne.

Publishes *Parcours* (Le Point Cardinal), a suite of twelve engravings that demonstrates a new development in his interest in alphabets and signs.

The *Cahiers de l'Herne* devotes a special issue to Michaux.

Travels to India, Thailand, and Cambodia.

1967 Begins experiments with acrylics, applying paint directly from the tube. Vaguely figurative, these works anticipate his 1968 series titled Arrachements (A Wrenching Tearing Away).[53]

Exhibition of works from 1946–66 at Galerie Le Point Cardinal, Paris. Exhibitions also held at Galerie-Librairie La Touriale, Marseille; Galleria del Naviglio, Milan; and Palazzo Grassi, Venice.

Travels to Lisbon, Miami, and the Yucatan.

1968 The May 1968 uprisings inspire Michaux to make large acrylic paintings, some of which are grouped under the title Arrachements.

Exhibition of paintings 1946–67 at INSCIR, Université de Rouen. Exhibitions also held at Galerie d'Art Moderne, Basel; Galerie Le Point Cardinal, Paris (with Pons and Viseux); and Galerie Edwin Engelberts, Geneva.

Travels to New York and Columbia.

Death of Jean Paulhan.

1969 Exhibition of a hundred drawings and paintings at the Von der Heydt Museum in Wuppertal, Germany. Visits the Musée des arts et de l'industrie, Saint-Étienne. Exhibition also held at Galerie de Buren, Stockholm, and Galerie Van de Loo, Munich.

Publishes *Façons d'endormi, façons d'éveillé* (Collection Le Point du Jour, Gallimard), Michaux's second book devoted to dreams, forty-five years after *Les Rêves et la jambe*.

1970 Travels to the Ivory Coast.

Exhibitions held at Galerie Maya, Brussels; Galerie Melisa, Lausanne; and Galerie Artek, Helsinki.

Writes preface to *La Calligraphie chinoise. Un art à quatre dimensions* by Léon Tchang Long-Yan. Republished separately as *Idéogrammes en Chine*, Montpellier (Fata Morgana) 1975.

1971 Exhibition of recent work at Galerie Le Point Cardinal, Paris, notably new "Batailles" ink works. Retrospective held at the Palais des Beaux-Arts de Charleroi; it travels to the Museum voor Schone Kunsten, Gent, and the Palais des Beaux-Arts, Brussels.

1972 Publishes *Émergences-Résurgences*, Geneva (Édition d'art Albert Skira), which traces the genesis of his art and contains reproductions of seventy-six paintings and drawings.

Retrospective held at the Kestner-Gesellschaft in Hanover.

1973 Exhibition held at Galerie S. Mamede, Lisbon.

Publishes *Moments. Traversées du temps* (Collection Le Point du Jour, Gallimard), which includes poems inspired by the art of Matta and others.

1974 Publishes *Par la voie des rythmes*, Montpellier (Fata Morgana), a book with reproductions of eighty-four drawings (including front and back covers) and no text. It is accompanied by a suite of twelve lithographs.

Exhibitions held at Galerie Le Point Cardinal, Paris, and Galerie Erker, Saint-Gall, Switzerland.

1975 Numerous exhibitions held worldwide: Galerie J. Davidson, Tours; Lefebre Gallery, New York; Galerie Melisa, Lausanne; Galerie Loeb, Bern; Galerie Gilles Gheerbrant, Montreal; and Moderna Museet, Stockholm.

1976 Major retrospective at the Fondation Maeght, Saint-Paul-de-Vence. Other retrospectives held at the Stadtmuseum, Graz, and the Museum des 20 Jahrhunderts, Vienna. Exhibitions held at Galerie Edwin Engelberts, Geneva; Galerie Maya, Brussels; and Galerie Le Point Cardinal, Paris.

Publishes *Les Ravagés*, Montpellier (Fata Morgana), written while considering paintings by the insane.

1977 Executes a number of small-scale oil paintings apparently related to earlier mescaline paintings. In his later years, works more with thicker media such as oil and acrylic, while continuing to work in ink and watercolor.

Exhibitions held at the Institut Français, Stockholm; Galerie Van de Loo, Munich; and Galerie Thomas Borgmann, Cologne.

1978 The largest retrospective to date is held at the Centre Georges Pompidou, Paris. Travels to the Solomon R. Guggenheim Museum, New York and the Musée d'art contemporain, Montréal. Exhibitions also held at Galerie Le Point Cardinal, Paris; Galerie Hubert Winter, Vienna; Galerie Heike Curtze, Vienna; and Galerie Gilles Gheerbrant, Montréal.

1979 Publishes *Saisir*, Montpellier (Fata Morgana), with reproductions of sixty-seven drawings.

Exhibitions held at Galerie Pudelko, Bonn, and Galerie A., Munich.

1980 Michaux injures his Achilles tendon while running for the train in Lausanne. Executes some small drawings in colored crayon while his foot is in a cast.

Exhibitions held at Galerie René Ziegler, Zürich, and Galerie Le Point Cardinal, Paris.

1981 Publishes *Comme un ensablement*, Montpellier (Fata Morgana), with serigraphs.[54]

Exhibitions held at Kaneko Art Gallery, Tokyo, and the Institut Français, Athens.

1982 Exhibitions held at Galerie Olsson, Stockholm; Galerie Le Point Cardinal, Paris; and Kaneko Art Gallery, Tokyo.

1983 Retrospective held at the Seibu Museum of Art, Tokyo. Exhibitions also held at the Musée Municipal de Kitakyushu; the Centre d'Exposition, Othsu; and Galerie Le Point Cardinal, Paris.

Publishes *Les Commencements, Dessins d'enfants, Essais d'enfants*, Montpellier (Fata Morgana).

1984 Publishes *Par des traits*, Montpellier (Fata Morgana), with reproductions of sixty-five drawings. It's the last book published during Michaux's lifetime.

Works on a series of small oil paintings.

Exhibitions held at Studio d'Arte, Turin; Galerie Le Point Cardinal, Paris; Galerie Astley, Skinsskatteberg; Galerie Blanche, Stockholm; Galerie Olsson, Stockholm; Musée de Valence, France; Edward Thorp Gallery, New York; and Galerie Artek, Helsinki.

Dies in a hospital following a heart attack on October 19.

NOTES

1. French-speaking people from Southern Belgium.

2. Belgian countryside bordering on Holland.

3. Norge in *Le Magazine littéraire*, June 1985, p. 22. Cited in Ouvry-Vial 1989, p. 43.

4. Ernest Hello was a late nineteenth-century mystical French Catholic writer who wrote against the "scientism" of his times. Ruysbroek is the great Dutch mystic of the fourteenth century.

5. Founded in the late nineteenth century, *Jeune Belgique* was a Belgian review that violently attacked the official literature of the time.

6. The examination that gives both a high-school diploma and entrance into university in French-speaking countries.

7. From "La Mer," *Épreuves, exorcismes 1940–1944*, Paris (Gallimard) 1999 (1945), p. 108.

8. The Surrealists would claim Lautréamont as their spiritual ancestor because of his *Chants de Maldoror*, published in 1868–69.

9. Franz Hellens was a Belgian writer with Surrealist sympathies; Jean Paulhan, writer and editor of *La Nouvelle Revue française*, was one of the most influential men in French letters in the first half of this century. He was to remain a close literary friend of Michaux's, his "man at Gallimard."

10. Cited in *Le Disque vert*, January 1925, p. 86.

11. Quoted by Patrick Waldberg, *Max Ernst*, Paris (Jean-Jacques Pauvert) 1958, p. 300. Cited in Guggenheim/Pompidou 1978, p. 11.

12. *Émergences-Résurgences*, trans. Elaine Harris in Guggenheim/Pompidou 1978, p. 14.

13. Quoted by Bellour and Tran 1998, p. 20.

14. From a letter to Jean Paulhan, May 15, 1928. Cited by Bellour and Tran 1998, p. 20.

15. From a letter to Claude Cahun, May 1934. Cited in Imbert 1999, p. 234.

16. Michaux expressed his interest in Lao-Tzeu in a letter to Jean Paulhan, August 9, 1932. Cited in Ouvry-Vial 1989, p. 94.

17. From a letter to Jean Paulhan written on board the *Kobe* en route to Japan, April 13, 1932. Cited in Imbert 1999, p. 234.

18. Cited in Ouvry-Vial 1989, p. 94. The Musée Guimet is devoted to Asian art.

19. Letter to Supervielle in Bellour and Tran 1998, p. 21.

20. Letter to Jean Paulhan, January 5, 1936. Cited in Ouvry-Vial 1989, p. 129.

21. Cited in Ouvry-Vial 1989, p. 151.

22. "Qui il est," *Peintures*, trans. Elaine Harris in Guggenheim/Pompidou 1978, p. 35.

23. Letter to Claude Cahun, August 1938. Cited in Imbert 1999, p. 236.

24. Cited in Ouvry-Vial 1989, p. 140.

25. "Peindre," *Passages*, 1950 (1963), trans. David Ball in Ball 1994, p. 309.

26. Small town on the Mediterranean.

27. Bellour and Tran 1998, p. 22.

28. Letter to Supervielle, July 13, 1941. Cited in Imbert 1999, p. 237.

29. Letter to Henri Parisot, November 30, 1941. Cited in Imbert 1999, p. 236.

30. Cited in Bellour and Tran 1998, p. 23.

31. Letter to Maurice Saillet, June 26, 1942. Cited in Ouvry-Vial 1989, p. 165.

32. Letter to Paulhan, January 1943. Cited in Ouvry-Vial 1989, p. 167.

33. "En pensant au phénomène de la peinture," *Peintures et dessins*, trans. David Ball in Ball 1994, p. 311.

34. *Passages* 1963, pp. 93–94.

35. *Émergences-Résurgences*, trans. Michael Fineberg in Guggenheim/Pompidou 1978, p. 60.

36. H.P. Roché, "Les Gouaches de Henri Michaux," *Henri Michaux*, exhib. cat., Paris, Galerie René Drouin, 1948.

37. From "Signes," *XXème Siècle* (1954). Cited in Guggenheim/Pompidou 1978, p. 69.

38. Postface, *Mouvements*, trans. Michael Fineberg. Cited in Guggenheim/Pompidou 1978, p. 71.

39. *Émergences-Résurgences*, trans. Elaine Harris and Michael Fineberg in Guggenheim/Pompidou 1978, p. 77.

40. Trans. John Ashbery in Galerie Daniel Cordier 1959. Cited in Guggenheim/Pompidou 1978, p. 80.

41. *Ibid.*

42. "Conversation avec Henri Michaux" (1959) in Alain Jouffroy, *Avec Henri Michaux*, Paris (Éditions du Rocher) 1992, p. 37.

43. "Vitesse et Tempo" (1957), trans. Michael Fineberg. Cited in Guggenheim/Pompidou 1978, p. 91.

44. *L'Homme gauche* in French, with a pun on *gauche*, clumsy, as well as the opposition to the usual right-handed man or right man.

45. *Botteghe oscure*, no. 20, October 1957.

46. Letter to Robert Bréchon, 1958. Cited in Imbert 1999, p. 239.

47. Cited in Bellour and Tran 1998, p. 26.

48. *Tel Quel*, no. 2, spring 1957. Republished as *Bras Cassé*, 1973.

49. "Vitesse et Tempo" was republished as "Dessiner l'écoulement du temps" (To Draw the Flow of Time), *Passages*, Paris (Gallimard) 1963.

50. "Conversation avec Henri Michaux," Jouffrey 1992, pp. 29–30.

51. *Mercure de France*, no. 1214, December 1964.

52. Preface, trans. John Ashbery, Robert Fraser Gallery 1963. Cited in Guggenheim/Pompidou 1978, p. 149.

53. Trans. Elaine Harris in Guggenheim/Pompidou 1978, p. 153.

54. Edition of 300: numbers 1–75 included six serigraphs. Numbers 76–300 contained four serigraphs.

BIBLIOGRAPHY

Leslie Jones

Bibliography of books, exhibition catalogues, and articles on Michaux. Dates in brackets refer to reprints. For works by Michaux, refer to the Chronology.

Books and Exhibition Catalogues

HENRI-ALEXIS BAATSCH, *Henri Michaux. Peinture et poésie*, Paris (Hazan) 1993

RAYMOND BELLOUR (ed.), *Henri Michaux. Cahiers de l'Herne*, no. 8, Paris (Éditions de l'Herne) 1966 (1983)

RENÉ BERTELÉ, *Henri Michaux*, "Poètes d'aujourd'hui" collection, Paris (Seghers) 1946 (1949) (1953) (1957) (1963) (1965) (1969) (1973) (1975)

GENEVIÈVE BONNEFOI, *Henri Michaux. Peintre*, Ginals (Abbaye de Beaulieu) 1976

ROBERT BRÉCHON, *Michaux*, Paris (Collection La Bibliothèque Idéale, Gallimard) 1959

ANNE BRUN, *Henri Michaux ou le corps halluciné*, "Les Empêcheurs de penser en rond" collection, Paris (Institut d'édition sanofi-synthelabo) 1999

MICHEL BUTOR, *Improvisations sur Henri Michaux*, Montpellier (Éditions Fata Morgana) 1985

LAURIE EDSON, *Henri Michaux and the Poetics of Movement*, Saratoga, California (Anma Libri) 1985

CLAUDE FINTZ, *Expérience esthétique et spirituelle chez Henri Michaux. La quête d'un savoir et d'une posture*, Paris (L'Harmattan) 1996

Henri Michaux, exhib. cat., Paris, Galerie René Drouin, 1948
[Texts by Michel Tapié, H.P. Roché, and Henri Michaux]

Henri Michaux. Encres, gouaches, dessins, exhib. cat., Paris, Galerie Daniel Cordier, October–November 1959
[Foreword by Henri Michaux]

Henri Michaux, exhib. cat., Silkeborg, Denmark, Silkeborg Museum, 1962
[Foreword by Asger Jorn]

Henri Michaux au Silkeborg Museum, exhib. cat., Silkeborg, Denmark, Silkeborg Museum, n.d.
[Publication of René Bertelé, "Les Propriétés d'Henri Michaux," in conjunction with above exhibition]

Henri Michaux. Œuvres récentes 1959–1962, exhib. cat., Paris, Galerie Daniel Cordier, 1962
[Text by Geneviève Bonnefoi, "L'Autre Langage"]

Henri Michaux. Peintures et dessins de 1937 à 1964, exhib. cat., Geneva, Galerie Motte, 1964

[Text by René Bertelé]

Henri Michaux, exhib. cat., Jean Delpech, Amsterdam, Stedelijk Museum, 1964
[Preface by Geneviève Bonnefoi-Brache and texts by René Bertelé and Henri Michaux]

Henri Michaux, exhib. cat., Paris, Musée national d'art moderne, 1965
[Foreword by Jean Cassou plus extracts from Henri Michaux's *Passages* and 1959 Cordier exhib. cat.]

Henri Michaux. Aquarelles, frottages, peintures à l'encre de Chine, aquarelles et gouaches, dessins de désagrégation, 1946–1966, exhib. cat., Geneva, Galerie Engelberts, 1966
[Essay by Jean Starobinski]

Henri Michaux. Choix d'œuvres des années 1946–1966, exhib. cat., Paris, Le Point Cardinal, 1967
[Foreword by Jean Grenier]

Henri Michaux. Peintures 1946–1967, exhib. cat., Rouen INSCIR, Université de Rouen, 1968
[Preface by Geneviève Bonnefoi, "Irréductible Michaux"]

Henri Michaux, exhib. cat., Wuppertal, von der Heydt-Museum, 1969
[Preface by René Bertelé]

Henri Michaux: rétrospective, exhib. cat., Charleroi, Belgium, Palais des Beaux-Arts, 1971
[Introduction by Jean Dypréau]

Henri Michaux, exhib. cat., Hannover (Kestner-Gesellschaft) 1972
[Texts by Wieland Schmied, Kurt Leohnard, and Henri Michaux]

Henri Michaux. Peintures, exhib. cat., H. Drude and F. Gaillard, Saint-Paul-de-Vence, Fondation Maeght, 1976
[Essays by Jacques Dupin, Geneviève Bonnefoi, and excerpts from Jean Starobinski (1966), G. Barrière (1974), Jean-Dominique Rey (1974), Edith Boissonas (1975), and Henri Michaux]

Henri Michaux, exhib. cat., New York, The Solomon R. Guggenheim Museum, and Paris, Centre Georges Pompidou, Musée national d'art moderne, 1978
[Preface by Pontus Hulten (in French edition); texts by Octavio Paz, Geneviève Bonnefoi, Henri-Alexis Baatsch, Edith Boissonas, and Jean Starobinski, and explanatory chapters by Agnès Angliviel de La Beaumelle, Alfred Pacquement, and G. Barrière; and conclusion by Thomas M. Messer (in English edition)]

Henri Michaux, exhib. cat., Tokyo, The Seibu Museum of Art, 1983
[Preface by Alfred Pacquement and texts by Makoto Ooka and Henri Michaux]

Henri Michaux, 1899–1984, exhib. cat., Geneva, Centre Genevois de Gravure Contemporaine, 1989
[Texts by Anne Patry, Paul Viaccoz, Jean Starobinski, Alfred Pacquement, and René Micha]

Henri Michaux, exhib. cat., Cologne, Galerie Karsten Greve, 1989
[Texts by Wieland Schmied, Max Bense, Francis Bacon, and Henri Michaux]

Henri Michaux, exhib. cat., Paris, Galerie Lelong, 1990
[Texts by Jean-Michel Maulpoix and Jacques Dupin]

Henri Michaux. Les livres illustrés, Paris (La Hune) 1993
[Texts by Maurice Imbert and Micheline Phankim]

Henri Michaux. Das bildnerische Werk, exhib. cat., Munich, Bayerishe Akademie der Schönen Künste, 1993
[Texts by Wieland Schmied, Octavia Paz, Kurt Leonhard, and Henri Michaux]

Henri Michaux. Œuvres choisies 1927–1984, exhib. cat., Marseille, Musée Cantini, Réunion des Musées Nationaux, 1993
[Essays by Florian Rodari, Claire Stoullig, Jean-Jacques Lebel, and Nicola Cendo; interview by Jean-Dominique Rey, and anthology including previously published essays by René Bertelé, Jacques Dupin, Asger Jorn, and Jean Starobinski]

Henri Michaux. Le langage du peintre le regard du poète, exhib. cat., Paris, Galerie Thessa Herold, 1994

"Michaux. Écrire et peindre," *Magazine littéraire*, no. 364, April 1998

Henri Michaux. Dibuixos mescalínics/dibujos mescalínicos, exhib. cat., Barcelona, Centre Cultural Tecla Sala, 1998
[Texts by Victoria Combalía, Jean-Jacques Lebel, and Henri Michaux]

Die Meskalinzeichnungen von Henri Michaux, exhib. cat., Neue Galerie Graz am Landesmuseum Joanneum, 1998
[Essays by Peter Weibel, Victoria Combalia, and Jean-Jacques Lebel]

Henri Michaux, exhib. cat., London, Whitechapel Art Gallery, 1999
[Essays by Vera Dickman and Caroline Douglas]

Henri Michaux. Le regard des autres, exhib. cat., Paris, Galerie Thessa Herold, 1999

ALAIN JOUFFROY, *Avec Henri Michaux*, Paris (Éditions du Rocher) 1992

KURT LEONHARD, *Henri Michaux*, trans. Anthony Kitzinger, Stuttgart (Verlag Gerd Hatje) Paris (Tisné), and London (Thames and Hudson) 1967

RAINER MICHAEL MASON and CHRISTOPHE CHERIX, *Henri Michaux. Les estampes. 1948–1984*, cat. raisonné, ed. Patrick Cramer, Geneva (Cabinet des estampes du Musée d'art et d'histoire) 1997
[Text by Bernard Gheerbrant]

JEAN-MICHEL MAULPOIX and FLORENCE DE LUSSY, *Henri Michaux. Peindre, composer, écrire*, exhib. cat., Paris, Bibliothèque nationale de France and Gallimard, 1999
[Texts by Maulpoix, Jean Louis Schefer, Jean Roudaut, Gérard Titus-Carmel, Pierre Alechinsky, Marc Le Bot, Pierre Boulez, Michel Collot, Maurice Blanchot, Florence de Lussy, and Gérard Macé, and a biography and bibliography by Maurice Imbert]

ALFRED PACQUEMENT, *Henri Michaux. Peintures*, Paris (Gallimard) 1983
[Essay by Raymond Bellour and an anthology of Michaux's texts on art]

YVES PEYRE, *En appel de visages*, Lagrasse (Verdier) 1983

RICHARD SIEBURTH, *Signs in Action Pound/Michaux*, New York (Red Dust) 1987

ADELIA V. WILLIAMS, *The Double Cipher: Encounter Between Word and Image in Bonnefoy, Tardieu and Michaux*, New York (Peter Lang) 1990

Articles

Pierre Alechinsky, "Plume et pinceau," *Pleine Marge*, no. 2, December 1985, pp. 7–20

Francis Bacon, interviewed by David Sylvester, BBC, 1962. Published in French as "Ce qu'a dit Francis Bacon à David Sylvester," *Derrière le miroir*, no. 162, November 1966, p. 21

Jean Burgos, "Michaux ou le plaisir du signe," *Pour une poétique de l'imaginaire*, Paris (Éditions du Seuil) 1982

Claude Fournet, "Questions de Peinture," *Promesse*, special edition on Michaux, nos. 19–20, fall–winter 1967, pp. 97–102

Jacques Kerno, "Approches d'une facture," *Promesse*, special edition on Michaux, nos. 19–20, fall–winter 1967, pp. 103–08

Max Loreau, "La Poésie, la peinture et le fondement du langage (H. Michaux)," in *La Peinture à l'œuvre et l'énigme du corps*, Paris (Gallimard) 1980, pp. 9–58

Catherine Mayaux, "*Dessins commentés* ou le fantôme du poète," in Pierre Grouix and Jean-Michel Maulpoix, eds., *Michaux: corps et savoir*, Fontenay-aux-Roses (ENS Éditions) 1998, pp. 17–32

Véra Mihaïlovich-Dickman, "Idéogrammes: l'apport de la Chine ou 'Voie par l'écriture,'" in Anne-Elisabeth Halpern and Véra Mihailovich-Dickman, eds., *Quelques orients d'Henri Michaux*, Paris (Éditions Findakly) 1996, pp. 159–90

Linda Orr, "The Sticky Figures of Henri Michaux," *Antaeus*, no. 54, spring 1985, pp. 189–95

Michael Peppiatt, "Henri Michaux: Painter Poet," *Art International* (Lugano), XVI, no. 1, January 20, 1972, pp. 28–33, 36

Carter Ratcliff, "Henri Michaux, Late Romantic," *Art in America*, LXXIII, no. 3, March 1985, pp. 146–49

Delphine Séris, "Les Meidosems: l'entreprise paradoxale du portrait," in Pierre Grouix and Jean-Michel Maulpoix, eds., *Michaux: corps et savoir*, Fontenay-aux-Roses (ENS Éditions) 1998, pp. 81–102

Sandrine Thiry, "Michaux et Dubuffet: rencontre de deux hommes du commun," in Pierre Grouix and Jean-Michel Maulpoix, eds., *Michaux: corps et savoir*, Fontenay-aux-Roses (ENS Éditions) 1998, pp. 297–324

CHECKLIST

Works are listed alphabetically by collection, and, thereafter, chronologically.
Height precedes width.

COLLECTION OF PIERRE ALECHINSKY, BOUGIVAL, FRANCE

Mescaline drawing, 1959 (p. 81)
Indian ink and watercolor on paper
11 × 7¼ in. (28 × 18.5 cm)

COLLECTION OF CLAUDE BERRI, PARIS

Untitled, 1925 (p. 13)
Indian ink on paper
12¼ × 18⅞ in. (31 × 48 cm)

Untitled (Lying Down [Couché]), 1938 (p. 21)
Gouache on black paper
12¾ × 19¾ in. (32.5 × 50 cm)

Untitled, 1938–39 (p. 19)
Gouache on black paper
11 × 11⅝ in. (28 × 29.5 cm)

Untitled, 1944 (p. 30)
Indian ink on paper
9½ × 12⅝ in. (24 × 32 cm)

Untitled, 1951 (p. 31)
Gouache on paper
9½ × 12⅝ in. (24 × 32 cm)

Untitled (Movements [Mouvements]), 1951 (p. 60)
Gouache on black paper
12⅝ × 9½ in. (32 × 24 cm)

Mescaline drawing, 1955 (p. 71)
Ink on paper
9 × 12¼ in. (23 × 31 cm)

Untitled, 1958 (p. 64)
Indian ink on paper
29½ × 41¼ in. (75 × 105 cm)

Mescaline drawing, c. 1958 (p. 82)
Indian ink on paper
19⅝ × 11 in. (50 × 28 cm)

Untitled, 1958 (p. 63)
Indian ink on paper
28½ × 41¼ in. (72.5 × 105 cm)

Mescaline drawing, 1958–59 (p. 83)
Ink on paper
20½ × 10⅝ in. (50 × 27 cm)

Untitled, 1961 (p. 109)
Indian ink on Japan paper
18⅛ × 24⅜ in. (46 × 62 cm)

Untitled, 1961 (p. 97)
Indian ink on paper
27¼ × 55½ in. (69 × 141 cm)

Untitled, 1962–63 (p. 119)
Indian ink on paper
18½ × 23⅝ in. (47 × 60 cm)

Untitled, 1966 (p. 117)
Ink on paper
12 × 15¾ in. (30.5 × 40 cm)

Post-mescaline drawing, 1966 (p. 127)
Ink on paper
12⅝ × 9½ in. (32 × 24 cm)

Untitled, 1968 (p. 133)
Indian ink on paper
29 × 41 in. (73.5 × 104 cm)

CABINET DES DESSINS DES MUSÉES D'ART ET
D'HISTOIRE, GENEVA

Untitled (Alphabet), 1944 (p. 38)
Indian ink on paper
12⅝ × 9½ in. (32 × 24 cm)

Untitled (Alphabet), 1944 (p. 42)
Indian ink on paper
12⅝ × 9½ in. (32 × 24 cm)

Untitled, 1945–46 (p. 33)
Watercolor and ink on paper
9½ × 12⅝ in. (24 × 32 cm)

Untitled (Movements [Mouvements]), 1950–51 (p. 54)
Indian ink on paper
12⅝ × 9½ in. (32 × 24 cm)

COLLECTION OF MRS. EDWIN ENGELBERTS, GENEVA

Untitled, 1942–44 (p. 24)
Indian ink on paper
9½ × 12⅝ in. (24 × 32 cm)

Untitled, 1942–44 (p. 25)
Indian ink on paper
9½ × 12⅝ in. (24 × 32 cm)

Untitled, 1942–44 (p. 26)
Indian ink on paper
12⅝ × 9½ in. (32 × 24 cm)

Untitled, 1944 (p. 28)
Indian ink on paper
9 × 12⅝ in. (23 × 32 cm)

Untitled, 1955 (p. 62)
Indian ink and yellow ink on paper
22 × 25½ in. (56 × 65 cm)

FONDATION MAEGHT, SAINT-PAUL-DE-VENCE, FRANCE

Untitled, 1960 (p. 89)
Indian ink on paper
29½ × 42½ in. (75 × 108 cm)

Untitled, 1968 (p. 134)
Indian ink on paper
29½ × 42½ in. (75 × 108 cm)

FONDS RÉGIONAL D'ART CONTEMPORAIN
DE PICARDIE, AMIENS, FRANCE

Untitled, 1960 (p. 92)
Indian ink on paper
29½ × 42½ in. (75 × 108 cm)

COLLECTION OF MR. AND MRS. CLAUDE FRONTISI

Untitled (*Movements* [*Mouvements*]), 1951 (p. 59)
Indian ink on paper
12⅝ × 9½ in. (32 × 24 cm)

GALERIE THESSA HEROLD, PARIS

Untitled, 1958–59 (p. 66)
Indian ink on paper
12¾ × 9¼ in. (32.5 × 23.5 cm)

Untitled, 1958–59 (p. 67)
Indian ink on paper
12¾ × 9¼ in. (32.5 × 23.5 cm)

Untitled, 1959 (p. 68)
Indian ink on paper
26⅜ × 19¼ in. (67 × 49 cm)

Untitled, 1959 (p. 69)
Indian ink and gouache on paper
26⅜ × 19¼ in. (67 × 49 cm)

Untitled, 1970 (p. 135)
Indian ink on paper
29½ × 42½ in. (75 × 105 cm)

Untitled, 1975 (not reproduced here)
Indian ink on paper
33½ × 59 in. (85 × 150 cm)

PRIVATE COLLECTION, COURTESY OF GALERIE THESSA
HEROLD, PARIS

Untitled (*Movements* [*Mouvements*]), 1951 (p. 57)
Indian ink on paper
12⅝ × 9½ in. (32 × 24 cm)

Untitled (*Movements* [*Mouvements*]), 1951 (p. 58)
Indian ink on paper
12⅝ × 9½ in. (32 × 24 cm)

Untitled, 1961 (pp. 98–99)
Indian ink on paper
18⅞ × 54¾ in. (48 × 139 cm)

COLLECTION OF MAURICE IMBERT, PARIS

Untitled (*The Blue Ladder* [*L'Échelle bleue*]), 1938 (p. 20)
Gouache on black paper
6¼ × 9⅝ in. (15.8 × 24.5 cm)

IVAM, INSTITUT VALENCIÀ D'ART MODERN, SPAIN

Untitled, 1961 (p. 104)
Indian ink and watercolor on paper
29½ × 42½ in. (75 × 108 cm)

Post-mescaline drawing, 1966 (p. 126)
Ink on paper
12¾ × 9 in. (32.5 × 23 cm)

JPC COLLECTION, GENEVA

Mescaline drawing, 1956 (p. 75)
Indian ink on paper
12⅝ × 9½ in. (32 × 24 cm)

Post-mescaline drawing, 1965 (p. 125)
Indian ink on paper
12½ × 9½ in. (31.5 × 24 cm)

Untitled, 1976 (p. 139)
Indian ink on paper
39⅜ × 59 in. (100 × 150 cm)

MUSÉE DE VALENCE, FRANCE

Post-mescaline drawing, 1966 (p. 128)
Indian ink on paper
15¾ × 10⅝ in. (40 × 27 cm)

Musée national d'art moderne, Centre Georges Pompidou, Paris

The Arena [L'Arène], 1938 (p. 22)
Pastel on black paper
12¾ × 9⅞ in. (32.4 × 25 cm)

Mescaline drawing, 1958 (p. 79)
Indian ink on paper
12⅜ × 9½ in. (31.4 × 24.1 cm)

Untitled, *c.* 1960 (p. 91)
Ink wash and watercolor on paper
19¾ × 22¼ in. (50 × 56.5 cm)

Untitled, 1961 (p. 111)
Indian ink on canvas
13¼ × 15½ in. (33.5 × 39.5 cm)

Untitled, 1961 (not reproduced here)
Indian ink on canvas
13⅛ × 15½ in. (33.4 × 39.6 cm)

Untitled (Painting in Indian ink [Peinture à l'encre de Chine]), 1962 (p. 115)
Indian ink on paper
18½ × 23⅝ in. (47 × 60 cm)

Untitled (Painting in Indian ink [Peinture à l'encre de Chine]), 1962 (p. 101)
Indian ink and sepia on paper
28⅛ × 41 in. (71.5 × 104 cm)

Inner Branchings [Arborescences intérieures], *c.* 1962–64 (p. 124)
Indian ink on paper
19¾ × 11¾ in. (50 × 30 cm)

The Museum of Modern Art, New York

Mescaline drawing, 1960 (p. 84)
Pen and ink on paper
12⅝ × 9½ in. (32 × 23.9 cm)

Untitled, 1960 (p. 90)
Brush and ink on paper
29⅜ × 42½ in. (74.5 × 107.8 cm)

Collection of Catherine Putman, Paris

Untitled, 1968 (p. 138)
Indian ink on paper
10¾ × 19¾ in. (50 × 27.5 cm)

Collection of Marie-Claude Tubiana, Paris

Untitled (The Three Suns [Les Trois Soleils]), 1958 (p. 65)
Indian ink on paper
28⅜ × 41¼ in. (72 × 105 cm)

Mescaline drawing, n.d. (p. 121)
Ink on paper
10½ × 7 in. (26.5 × 18 cm)

Private collections

Alphabet, 1927 (pp. 14–15)
Ink on paper
14¼ × 10¼ in. (36 × 26 cm)

Narration, 1927 (p. 16)
Indian ink on paper
14⅝ × 10⅝ (37 × 27 cm)

Untitled (Tropical Tree [Arbre des tropiques]), 1937 (p. 18)
Gouache on black paper
9½ × 12⅝ in. (24 × 32 cm)

Untitled (Alphabet), 1944 (p. 37)
Indian ink on paper
12⅝ × 9½ in. (32 × 24 cm)

Untitled (Alphabet), 1944 (p. 39)
Indian ink on paper
12⅝ × 9½ in. (32 × 24 cm)

Untitled (Alphabet), 1944 (p. 40)
Indian ink on paper
12⅝ × 9½ in. (32 × 24 cm)

Untitled (Alphabet), 1944 (p. 41)
Indian ink on paper
12⅝ × 9½ in. (32 × 24 cm)

Untitled (Alphabet), 1944 (p. 43)
Indian ink on paper
12⅝ × 9½ in. (32 × 24 cm)

Untitled, 1944 (p. 27)
Indian ink on paper
12⅝ × 9½ in. (32 × 24 cm)

Untitled, 1945–46 (p. 29)
Watercolor and ink on paper
9⅞ × 12¾ in. (25 × 32.5 cm)

Untitled, 1945–46 (p. 32)
Watercolor and ink on paper
9¾ × 13 in. (25 × 33 cm)

Untitled, 1945–46 (p. 34)
Watercolor and ink on paper
9⅞ × 12¾ in. (25 × 32.5 cm)

Untitled, 1945–46 (p. 35)
Indian ink on paper
9½ × 12⅝ in. (24 × 32 cm)

Untitled (Movements [Mouvements]), 1950–51 (p. 45)
Ink on paper
12⅝ × 9½ in. (32 × 24 cm)

Untitled (Movements [Mouvements]), 1950–51 (p. 46)
Ink on paper
12⅝ × 9½ in. (32 × 24 cm)

Untitled (*Movements* [*Mouvements*]), 1950–51 (p. 47)
Indian ink on paper
12⅝ × 9½ in. (32 × 24 cm)

Untitled (*Movements* [*Mouvements*]), 1950–51 (p. 48)
Indian ink on paper
12⅝ × 9½ in. (32 × 24 cm)

Untitled (*Movements* [*Mouvements*]), 1950–51 (p. 49)
Indian ink on paper
12⅝ × 9½ in. (32 × 24 cm)

Untitled (*Movements* [*Mouvements*]), 1950–51 (p. 50)
Indian ink on paper
12⅝ × 9½ in. (32 × 24 cm)

Untitled (*Movements* [*Mouvements*]), 1950–51 (p. 51)
Indian ink on paper
12⅝ × 9½ in. (32 × 24 cm)

Untitled (*Movements* [*Mouvements*]), 1950–51 (p. 52)
Indian ink on paper
12⅝ × 9½ in. (32 × 24 cm)

Untitled (*Movements* [*Mouvements*]), 1950–51 (p. 53)
Indian ink on paper
12⅝ × 9½ in. (32 × 24 cm)

Untitled (*Movements* [*Mouvements*]), 1950–51 (p. 55)
Indian ink on paper
12⅝ × 9½ in. (32 × 24 cm)

Untitled (*Movements* [*Mouvements*]), 1950–51 (p. 56)
Indian ink on paper
12⅝ × 9½ in. (32 × 24 cm)

Untitled, 1951 (not reproduced here)
Indian ink on paper
42⅛ × 29½ in. (107 × 75 cm)

Mescaline drawing, 1955 (p. 72)
Indian ink on paper
12⅝ × 9½ in. (32 × 24 cm)

Mescaline drawing, *c.* 1956 (p. 76)
Pencil on paper
15¾ × 10⅝ in. (40 × 27 cm)

Mescaline drawing, *c.* 1956 (p. 77)
Pencil on paper
15¾ × 10⅝ in. (40 × 27 cm)

Mescaline drawing, 1956 (p. 74)
Indian ink on paper
15⅜ × 10¼ in. (39 × 26 cm)

Psilocybin drawing, 1956 (p. 73)
Indian ink on paper
12⅝ × 9½ in. (32 × 24 cm)

Mescaline drawing, 1956–58 (p. 78)
Colored pencil on paper
16¼ × 12⅝ in. (41.5 × 32 cm)

Mescaline drawing, 1957 (p. 80)
Indian ink on paper
15⅜ × 10¼ in. (39 × 26 cm)

Untitled, 1959 (p. 87)
Brown and black ink on paper
29½ × 41¾ in. (75 × 106 cm)

Untitled, 1959 (p. 88)
Indian ink on paper
29½ × 42⅛ in. (75 × 108 cm)

Untitled, 1960 (pp. 94–95)
Indian ink on paper
25½ × 55⅛ in. (65 × 140 cm)

Untitled, 1960 (pp. 96–97)
Indian ink on paper
29½ × 42⅛ in. (75 × 107 cm)

Untitled, *c.* 1961 (p. 113)
Indian ink on paper
19¾ × 26 in. (50 × 66 cm)

Untitled, 1961 (p. 100)
Indian ink on paper
29½ × 42⅛ in. (75 × 107 cm)

Untitled, 1961 (p. 108)
Indian ink on canvas
13¾ × 16⅛ in. (35 × 41 cm)

Untitled, 1961 (p. 110)
Indian ink on canvas
13¾ × 15¾ in. (35 × 40 cm)

Untitled, 1961 (p. 112)
Indian ink on canvas
13½ × 15¾ in. (34.5 × 40 cm)

Untitled, 1961–62 (p. 107)
Ink on Japanese paper
9⅞ × 20½ in. (25 × 57 cm)
9⅞ × 21¼ in. (25 × 54 cm)
9⅞ × 18½ in. (25 × 47 cm)

Untitled (*Painting in Indian ink* [*Peinture à l'encre de Chine*]), 1962 (p. 102)
Indian ink on paper
19¼ × 23⅝ in. (49 × 60 cm)

Untitled, 1962 (p. 114)
Watercolor and ink on paper
19¼ × 25⅜ in. (49 × 64.5 cm)

Untitled (*Painting in Indian ink* [*Peinture à l'encre de Chine*]), 1962 (p. 103)
Indian ink and sepia on paper
19¾ × 25½ in. (50 × 65 cm)

Untitled, 1963 (p. 116)
Indian ink on paper
18⅞ × 23⅝ in. (48 × 60 cm)

Untitled, 1963 (p. 118)
Indian ink and sepia on paper
12⅝ × 16½ in. (32 × 42 cm)

Post-mescaline drawing, *c*. 1969 (p. 129)
Indian ink and colored ink on paper
12¼ × 8¾ in. (31 × 22 cm)

Post-mescaline drawing, *c*. 1969 (p. 130)
Indian ink and colored ink on paper
14¾ × 11 in. (38 × 28 cm)

Untitled, *c*. 1970 (p. 156)
Indian ink on paper
13⅜ × 26¾ in. (34 × 68 cm)

Untitled, *c*. 1970 (p. 136)
Indian ink and acrylic on paper
29⅛ × 41¾ in. (74 × 106 cm)

Untitled, 1973 (p. 137)
Ink and acrylic on paper
22½ × 30⅜ in. (57 × 77 cm)

Untitled, 1974 (p. 157)
Indian ink on paper
14¼ × 27½ in. (36 × 70 cm)

Untitled (*By Way of Rhythms* [*Par la voie des rythmes*]), 1974 (p. 150)
Ink on paper
12⅝ × 10¼ in. (34 × 26 cm)

Untitled (*By Way of Rhythms* [*Par la voie des rythmes*]), 1974 (p. 151)
Ink on paper
12⅝ × 10¼ in. (34 × 26 cm)

Untitled (*By Way of Rhythms* [*Par la voie des rythmes*]), 1974 (p. 146)
Ink on paper
12¾ × 10¼ in. (32.5 × 26 cm)

Untitled (*By Way of Rhythms* [*Par la voie des rythmes*]), 1974 (p. 147)
Ink on paper
12¾ × 10¼ in. (32.5 × 26 cm)

Untitled (*By Way of Rhythms* [*Par la voie des rythmes*]), 1974 (p. 154)
Ink on paper
13 × 10¼ in. (33 × 26 cm)

Untitled (*By Way of Rhythms* [*Par la voie des rythmes*]), 1974 (p. 155)
Ink on paper
13 × 10¼ in. (33 × 26 cm)

Untitled (*By Way of Rhythms* [*Par la voie des rythmes*]), 1974 (p. 144)
Ink on paper
17⅛ × 12⅜ in. (43.5 × 31.5 cm)

Untitled (*By Way of Rhythms* [*Par la voie des rythmes*]), 1974 (p. 145)
Ink on paper
17⅛ × 12⅜ in. (43.5 × 31.5 cm)

Untitled (*By Way of Rhythms* [*Par la voie des rythmes*]), 1974 (p. 148)
Ink on paper
12¾ × 10¼ in. (32.5 × 26 cm)

Untitled (*By Way of Rhythms* [*Par la voie des rythmes*]), 1974 (p. 149)
Ink on paper
12¾ × 10¼ in. (32.5 × 26 cm)

Untitled (*By Way of Rhythms* [*Par la voie des rythmes*]), 1974 (p. 152)
Ink on paper
12¾ × 10¼ in. (32.5 × 26 cm)

Untitled (*By Way of Rhythms* [*Par la voie des rythmes*]), 1974 (p. 153)
Ink on paper
12¾ × 10¼ in. (32.5 × 26 cm)

Untitled, *c*. 1975 (p. 140)
Indian ink on paper
37 × 59 in. (94 × 150 cm)

Untitled, 1975 (pp. 142–43)
Indian ink on paper
33½ × 59 in. (85 × 150 cm)

Untitled (*Procession of Monks, or Rather of Mandarins* [*Défilé de moines ou bien de mandarins*]), 1977 (p. 160)
Oil on canvas
7½ × 10½ in. (19.5 × 27 cm)

Untitled, 1980 (p. 158)
Indian ink on Japanese paper, mounted on paper
Each sheet 8 × 27½ in. (19 × 70 cm)

Untitled, 1981 (p. 159)
Indian ink, acrylic, and pencil on paper
19¾ × 25½ in. (50 × 65 cm)

Mescaline drawing, n.d. (p. 122)
Indian ink on paper
19¾ × 10⅞ in. (50 × 27.5 cm)

Mescaline drawing, n.d. (p. 123)
Indian ink on paper
14½ × 10¼ in. (36.8 × 26 cm)

Untitled (*Cave* [*Caverne*]), n.d. (p. 141)
Indian ink on paper
23⅝ × 33⅞ in. (60 × 86 cm)

Lenders to the Exhibition

Pierre Alechinsky, Bougival, France; Claude Berri, Paris; Cabinet des dessins des Musées d'art et d'histoire, Geneva; Mrs. Edwin Engelberts, Geneva; Fondation Maeght, Saint-Paul-de-Vence, France; Fonds régional d'art contemporain, Picardie, France; Mr. and Mrs. Claude Frontisi; Galerie Thessa Herold, Paris; Maurice Imbert, Paris; IVAM, Institut Valencià d'Art Modern, Spain; JPC Collection, Geneva; Musée de Valence, France; Musée national d'art moderne, Centre Georges Pompidou, Paris; The Museum of Modern Art, New York; Catherine Putman, Paris; and Marie-Claude Tubiana, Paris. Our gratitude is also extended to those lenders who wish to remain anonymous.

Photograph Credits

When available, the names of the photographers are provided in parentheses.

Pierre Alechinsky, Bougival, France (A. Morin): p. 81
Claude Berri, Paris (Cathy Carver): pp. 13, 19, 21, 30, 31, 60, 63, 64, 71, 82, 83, 96–97, 109,
117, 119, 127, 133
Cabinet des dessins des Musées d'art et d'histoire, Geneva (Cathy Carver): pp. 33, 38, 42, 54
Mrs Edwin Engelberts, Geneva (Claude Mercier): pp. 24–26, 28, 62
Fondation Maeght, Saint-Paul-de-Vence, France (Claude Germain): pp. 89, 134
Fonds régional d'art contemporain, Picardie, France (André Morin): p. 92
Galerie Thessa Herold, Paris (Cathy Carver): pp. 66, 67, 69, 135
Maurice Imbert, Paris (Cathy Carver): p. 20
IVAM, Institut Valencià d'Art Modern, Spain (Juan Garcia Rosell): pp. 104, 126
JPC Collection, Geneva: pp. 75, 125, 139
Musée de Valence, France (Philippe Peliot): p. 128
Musée national d'art moderne, Centre Georges Pompidou, Paris (Jacques Faujour, Philippe
Migeat, Adam Rzepka): pp. 22, 79, 91, 101, 111, 115, 124
The Museum of Modern Art, New York: pp. 84, 90
Catherine Putman, Paris (Cathy Carver): p. 138
Private collections (Cathy Carver, Patrick Lorette, Piotr Trawinksi): pp. 14–16, 18, 27, 29, 32,
34, 35, 37, 39–41, 43, 45–53, 55–59, 72–74, 76–78, 80, 87, 88, 93–95, 98–100, 102, 103, 107,
108, 110, 112–14, 116, 118, 122, 123, 129, 130, 136, 137, 140–60
Marie-Claude Tubiana, Paris (Cathy Carver): pp. 65, 121

Photograph of Michaux on p. 2 by Claude Cahun, courtesy of Galerie Berggruen, Paris

First published in 2000 by

Merrell Publishers Limited
42 Southwark Street
London SE1 1UN
www.merrellpublishers.com

and

The Drawing Center
35 Wooster Street
New York, New York 10013

Distributed in the USA and Canada by Rizzoli International Publications, Inc.
through St. Martin's Press, 175 Fifth Avenue, New York, New York 10010

United States Library of Congress Catalogue Card Number:
00-133022

British Library Cataloguing-in-Publication Data
Untitled passages by Henri Michaux
1.Michaux, Henri, 1899–1984 – Exhibitions 2.Drawing, French – Exhibitions 3.Drawing – 20th Century – Exhibitions
I.Bellour, Raymond II.Zegher, Catherine de
741.9'44

ISBN 1 85894 120 2

Front cover, top: *Untitled*, 1968 (FONDATION MAEGHT, SAINT-PAUL-DE-VENCE, FRANCE)

Front cover, bottom: *Untitled*, 1960 (FONDATION MAEGHT, SAINT-PAUL-DE-VENCE, FRANCE)

Back cover: Portrait of Henri Michaux, anonymous, n.d.

Frontispiece: Henri Michaux photographed by Claude Cahun, n.d. (COURTESY OF GALERIE BERGGRUEN, PARIS)

Edited by Catherine de Zegher
Copy-edited by Iain Ross
Designed by Luc Derycke
Coordinated by Katie Dyer
Produced by Merrell Publishers Limited
Printed and bound in Italy

The text by Laurent Jenny was translated by Alyson Waters. The texts by Florian Rodari and Raymond Bellour were translated by Christine Schmiedel and Richard Sieburth.

DATE DUE

INTERLIBRARY LOAN			
JUL 1 1 2001			
			Printed in USA